SCALING SILICON VALLEY STYLE—VOL.I

SCALING
SILICON VALLEY STYLE

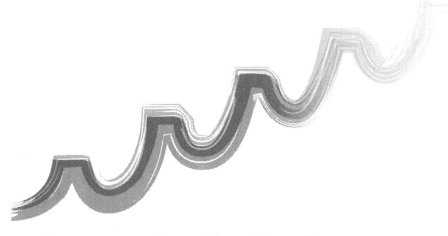

GROWING BIG BUT NOT CORPORATE

ROLAND SIEBELINK
& DOUG MILLER

VOL. I—THE PLAYBOOK FOR THE MID-STAGE STARTUP. FROM SEED FUNDING TO SERIES C

Scaling Silicon Valley Style. Growing Big Without Growing Corporate.
Vol. I: The Playbook for the Mid-Stage Startup. From Seed Funding to Series C.

Illustrations classicdjinn

Proofreading Marc Chauvet

Charts and typesetting Ángel Prieto Silva

Overall support Chuck Cabugoy

Scaleup Allies LLC
101 California Street Suite 2710
San Francisco CA 94111
United States of America
Office phone +1-415-633-8814

ISBN-13: 978-1-5351-1346-5 | ISBN-10: 1-5351-1346-4

22 21 19 18   03 04 05 06 07 08 09

www.scalingsiliconvalleystyle.com
www.rolandsiebelink.com
www.scaleupallies.com

To our loving families
who are always there to support us
in our work and lives.

"I wish someone had a methodology as simple as THE LEAN STARTUP for how to scale my company"

"PATRICK" QUOTED BY STEVE BLANK

Contents

CONTENTS

List of Figures

List of Tables

13

Preface–by Doug Miller

Roland and I wrote this book to talk about the amazing journeys that tech startups embark on. The journeys they travel after they have found their initial success.

> A few customers are buying the product, loving the results, and referring new clients. These companies are growing very, very fast to serve an exploding demand. This growth leads to an IPO. The founders make hundreds of millions of dollars. VCs make giant multiples on their returns. Most early employees get downpayments on a home. And the company becomes successful for decades.

This is the conventional expectation of every founder when they start their venture. But this path is the exception, not the rule. I hope that this book gives some new answers why. And that it provokes venture leadership to address the following questions:

- After initial success, why do so many startups fail?

- Why do so many companies disappear after raising series A, never to be heard from again?

- Why are so many founders forced out and replaced before the IPO?

- Why do companies with so much promise fail and go out of business?

- Why do second movers overtake first movers in so many markets?

I am a scarred veteran of the 2000 dotcom bubble burst. My company eGroups was set to go public mere weeks before the bubble popped. We later sold it to Yahoo!.

I have gotten to ring the NASDAQ bell when Rocket Fuel went public. (This was in a TV studio on Times Square, there is no actual trading floor). I experienced Rocket Fuel's challenges leading to a private exit four years later. These amazing accomplishments and bitter losses led me to think. How and why do companies in Silicon Valley fail and thrive.

For 20 years, I have led and driven forward tech businesses with innovation and curiosity. Believing that *enough smart people* who are *aligned* around *the right problems* can do anything. And then I got exposed to Gazelles' coaches and the *Scaling Up* method. (Harnish, 2014)

I began to understand that I had the right approach. But that there were more repeatable and proven ways to get the key components of:

- Enough "Smart People"

- Aligned

- Around the "Right Problems"

It was on a January 13th that I entered a conference room with many of my leadership peers. We were embarking on a turnaround of a company that had lost its wild success track. I was looking forward to working with my peers. But in my heart of hearts, I was sure that these three days were going to be an expensive waste of resources and time. I was certain everyone in the room already knew what we needed to do. Adjusting our business model, getting new products to market. And providing our customers with smooth onboarding and great service.

It was in these three days that I first learned about *Scaling Up*. I started reexamining how to build and grow successful businesses. The method slowly but steadily undermined my initial skepticism. We used individual tools to brainstorm and then a clear process to share and rank our ideas. We agreed on priorities, accountability, and action plans.

I stopped being a skeptic when it became clear that this was no ordinary three day planning meeting. Where we would end with no follow-through as the grind of our day-to-day business distracted everyone.

At the end of the session, we had pulled everything together into a One Page Strategic Plan 0.1. We had subteams accountable for deliverables. We scheduled weekly team meetings and monthly reporting to the executive staff. We agreed on a dashboard to keep the outcomes of our priorities visible at all times. We even received ongoing coaching to hold each of us accountable to the process and the outcomes.

Many people got excited about *Scaling Up* with me. Not too structured a person, my embrace of this rigorous approach surprised people. But I saw how the structure unleashed teams all across the company to align and drive results.

My co-author Roland Siebelink became a Gazelles Certified Coach during this meeting. He and I spent hours and hours in and out of work

Strategy: One-Page Strategic Plan (OPSP)

Organization Name:

People (Reputation Drivers)

Employees	Customers	Shareholders
1.	1.	1.
2.	2.	2.
3.	3.	3.

CORE VALUES/BELIEFS (Should/Shouldn't)	PURPOSE (Why)	TARGETS (3-5 YRS.) (Where)		GOALS (1 YR.) (What)	
		Future Date		Yr. Ending	
		Revenues		Revenues	
		Profit		Profit	
		Mkt. Cap./Cash		Mkt. Cap.	
		Sandbox		Gross Margin	
				Cash	
				A/R Days	
				Inv. Days	
				Rev./Emp.	

Actions (To Live Values, Purposes, BHAG®)	Key Thrusts/Capabilities	Key Initiatives
1	1	1
2	2	2
3	3	3
4	4	4
5	5	5

Profit per X	Brand Promise KPIs	Critical #: People or B/S
		○
		○
		○ Between green and red
		○

BHAG®	Brand Promises	Critical #: Process or P/L
		○
		○
		○ Between green and red
		○

Strengths/Core Competencies	Weaknesses
1.	1.
2.	2.
3.	3.

Figure 0.1: Gazelles One Page Strategic Plan

Gazelles
GROWING LEADERS – GROWING COMPANIES

Process (Productivity Drivers)

Make/Buy
1. _____
2. _____
3. _____

Sell
1. _____
2. _____
3. _____

Record Keeping
1. _____
2. _____
3. _____

ACTIONS (How)	THEME (Qtr./Annual)	YOUR ACCOUNTABILITY (Who/When)

Qtr. #	
Revenues	
Profit	
Mkt. Cap.	
Gross Margin	
Cash	
A/R Days	
Inv. Days	
Rev./Emp.	

Deadline	
Measurable Target/Critical #	

Theme Name

Your KPIs		Goal
1		
2		
3		

Rocks

		Who
1		
2		
3		
4		
5		

Scoreboard Design
Describe and/or sketch your design in this space

Your Quarterly Priorities		Due
1		
2		
3		
4		
5		

Critical #: People or B/S
- ⬤
- ⬤
- ◯ Between green and red
- ⬤

Celebration

Critical #: People or B/S
- ⬤
- ⬤
- ◯ Between green and red
- ⬤

Critical #: Process or P/L
- ⬤
- ⬤
- ◯ Between green and red
- ⬤

Reward

Critical #: Process or P/L
- ⬤
- ⬤
- ◯ Between green and red
- ⬤

Trends

1. _____
2. _____
3. _____
4. _____
5. _____
6. _____

talking how well this approach worked for the tech company we worked at. But we also wondered about Gazelles' "one size fits all" for different industries. And how Scaling Up could align better to wisdom learned in Silicon Valley scaleups.

These discussions were the origin of the concepts behind *Scaling Silicon Valley Style.* In our experience, tech companies have a unique challenge. Distinct capital investment processes and a need to grow very fast. A drive to be innovative, yet to disrupt entire markets. And enormous numbers of people to hire while maintaining a strong culture.

It was obvious. To embrace *Scaling Up*, tech companies needed more specific guidance.

1. We knew how many tech companies have leaders who are early in their careers. This led us to think about a phased curriculum, like in college.

2. We also saw an intense need to stop using the word "startup" so broadly. What works for four people in a garage is hardly going to work for 200 people spread around the world. The four-people *startup* only need apply new technology to a broad set of problems. The 200-people organization better have customers, revenue, priorities and a clear direction. It is hardly a startup in the same sense.

In this book we refer to companies "post start up" as scaleups. Scale-ups need a different way of leading than both startups and incumbents. And we also think that recipe for success changes as the scaleup moves from startup to incumbent.

This is why we organized this book (and its sequel) around four distinct phases of scaleup maturity. Each touches on revenue, marketing, sales, people, profits, leadership, and other company aspects.

These four stages, which we will cover in two books, align roughly with the typical rounds of VC funding. Even so, the growth in funding does not define each stage. Other growth aspects matter as much or more. Growth in revenue. Growth in volume. Growth in hiring. Growth in maturity. Growth in outcomes. This is why decided to label the four stages of scale-ups:

1. Freshman Scaleups

2. Sophomore Scaleups

3. Junior Scaleups

4. Senior Scaleups

In each phase, finding enough "smart people" is a challenge. Even more so as a person attracted to a freshman scaleup may not like a senior scaleup. You even have to redefine "smart" across functional departments, skill, and experience levels. In all stages, recruiting, nurturing, and retention of talent is important. Yet each will look very different as a company scales up. Furthermore, we have all seen top performers early in the company get too much leeway in later stages. They can become destructive to the company, its employees and its customers.

The most obvious challenge as you scale up is alignment. People, customers, and functions keep growing and focusing on their own needs. Ensuring alignment to drive the business forward becomes more and more challenging. What worked before stops working. Employees can become outright aggressive at defending their "turf". This is an acute problem when experienced leaders come in without domain expertise. Early employees can become disillusioned as professional managers take over the business.

Finally, the biggest challenge for scaleups is to define the "right problems". And to be specific what the most important problems are right now, and over the next twelve months. Creating new solutions to any challenge at the speed of thought works well across 30 people. But this same innovation and constant pivoting can paralyze a 120-person organization. Too often, we see everyone dropping what they are doing. The urgent gets prioritized over the important.

I find that it is as critical to list what *is not* a priority as much as it is to list what *is*. Leadership teams need to make sure the employees across scaleups know:

1. everything they considered for prioritization,

2. what is a priority now,

3. what is *not* a priority now.

It is critical to communicate in this way what is and is not "above the line". Only this will empower people across sales, service, product, and engineering to say "NO!" No to any request that is not a clear priority. Without people taking the refusal personally.

Clarity on what the organization heard but did not rank high enough creates trust. Trust that leadership is making informed decisions. That it weighs trade-offs across the many opportunities facing the business.

In the end, this book is about leadership. And how leadership needs to respond to the changing needs of a scaleup. Scaling up any organization is about constant change and innovation. But growing revenue revenue and employees is not enough. In the end, the emphasis leadership lays in each stage drives sustainable success.

I hope every (potential) tech startup founder/CEO reads this book and the sequel that will come out next year. So that he or she is prepared to adapt their approach to the business as it scales. Yet I also hope it reaches beyond this narrow audience of just founder/CEOs. Every scaleup executive needs to know about these changing requirements. To understand how the demands on their leadership will change as the scaleup grows. I expect this book to help them think ahead of how to adapt and respond to these changing needs.

I also hope this book and its key concepts will be helpful to all of us who have failed in a role. Or who have had a company or role outgrow our skills or interests. At one time or another we have all failed to adapt fast enough to changes in our professional lives. I hope this provides us all with guidance to adapt successfully in future endeavors.

The final audience I hope reads this book is anyone who is an employee at a fast-growing company. In my early 20s I was employee #35 at eGroups. I remember our merger with Onelist, our cancelled IPO in 2000, and later acquisition by Yahoo!. All this happened within 20 months! I remember my confusion as things changed. How I longed for the "good old days" (of four weeks ago) before we moved offices or completed a merger. Scaleup employees, I hope this book helps you see why the company you love is changing before your eyes. And why both you and your leaders need to change your expectations constantly. That it is the only way to thrive in the exciting scaleup work environment.

I want to thank my many, many mentors across my career. Thanks to Randy, JT, and Simon for introducing me to *Scaling Up*. And thanks most critically to my co-author Roland Siebelink. His intellect and experience drove most of the thought leadership in the book. Roland has a great ability to synthesize the success of the scaleups he has worked with. I am happy to have drawn his insights out with with some probing questions. Last but not least I want to thank my wife and children. They let me lock myself away in my bedroom to work on and refine this book.

I truly hope you enjoy learning how to "Scale Silicon Valley Style". Go ahead and drive amazing results for your organization and your career.

Pacifica
March 2018

Acknowledgements

This book would have never come into being without the wealth of learnings I (Roland) have been grateful to gain from so many scaleup executives over so many years. I want to thank in particular:

- Laurence, Neil, Kevin, Mats, Nigel, Mel, Jonas, Derek, Charles, Sam, Tommy, Anna and all other Leadership team members of VGW;

- Cris, Flavio, Daniel, Andreas, Andrada, Alberto, Bobbi, Corey, Filip, Matthew and Philippe at Beekeeper;

- Rik, Loren, Mike, Renee, Mark, Chris, Dan, Beth and Jeff at InRule;

- George, Richard, Jarvis, Rex, Corinn, JoAnn, Peter, Yasmine, JT, Nikolai, Beth, Tota, Lee, Renata, Glenn, Sue, Sam, Jessie, Dan, Mark, Lindsey, Jack, Corey, Kristina, Amy, Pauline, Jon, Chris, Christine, Mansi, Matt, Millie, Chai, Patrick and the many many other colleagues I enjoyed working with at Rocket Fuel over the years;

- Urs, Knut, Philip, Martin, Christoph, Pascal, Marko, Daniel, Bettina and Jörg at Bluewin/Swisscom;

- Chuck, Dave, Dino, Frits, Chris, Gino, Christo, Jeroen, Peter, Evi, Sophie, Wim, Nicolas, Danny, Jan and—passed so early—Peter V at Telenet;

- Gazelles coaches Verne, Keith, Bill, Shannon, Ron, Sean and the many others whom I have learned so much from over the years;

- My MBA friends Carlos, Diego, De la Rey, Alex, Mirko, Jesús, Valdur, Yoav, Marc, Ariel, Thaniya, Thomas, James, Marie, Yudi, Paco, Christian, Brian and Javier and the many others I didn't mention;

- My San Francisco friends Peter and Agata, Alex and Michael, Jim and Andrea, Billy and Charlie, Thomas, Kevin, Ronald and Carla, Elise and Jihyun, Abraham, Gino, Eric, Hou, Jon, Julian, André, Leigh and Paul, Monika, Phil;

- My Benelux friends Alexander and Gaby, Dennis, Martijn and Andrea, Anne, Mark, Emmanuel, Peter and Elke;

- Anyone I have forgotten to mention above even though they occupy an important place in my life, with sincere apologies!

- And of course my family Guus and Hierma, Esther and Wilbert, Luuk and Femke, Jeroen and Anja, Hanne and Senne.

But most of all I want to thank my husband Aki and our doggie Frits, who have shown enormous patience while I struggled to get this book done. Love you!

Beyond Product-Market-Fit

1.1 Situation: Startups Hitting Traction

DOUG: I have enjoyed collaborating with you on this book, Roland! It takes place in the land of technology startups, does it not?

ROLAND: Yes, our story will be about startups that "take off." From the first sales, through several growth phases, up to a corporate incumbent.

In other words, it is about the scaling journey that successful startups go through. And what they need to change and learn to remain successful through all these stages.

DOUG: That covers a different territory than the usual startup manual...

ROLAND: It does. In fact, consider this book the sequel to *Lean Startup* (Ries, 2011). The standard playbook for startups *before* product-market-fit. Early-stage founders reach initial market success with *Lean Startup*.

"A scaleup is a former startup
looking to turn product-market-fit
into product-market-dominance"

ROLAND SIEBELINK

Mid-stage founders can use this book to up their game and keep banking success after success.

DOUG: Traditional startup manuals only bring founders so far?

ROLAND: Traditional startup manuals concentrate on the first stage of the entrepreneurial journey. On bringing founders from an initial idea to a successful product with market traction.

DOUG: The famous milestone of *product-market-fit*.

ROLAND: Yes, indeed. All traditional startup manuals, entrepreneurial university courses or incubators do the same. They help founders turn their ideas into product-market-fit (Griffin, 2017).

With this book, our mission is different. We start from product-market-fit and help entrepreneurs turn that into *product-market-dominance*. We help turn fledgling startups with initial market response into true disruptors. Scaleups that have massive market impact. That provide major growth opportunities for its employees. And that generate manifold returns to the investors backing them in their early days.

DOUG: Wait, are you trying to square the circle between startup ways and corporate ways?

Table 1.1: Scaleups—Between Startups and Incumbents

Aspect	Tech Startup	Tech Scaleup	Tech "Stayup" (Incumbent)
Key goal	Product-Market-Fit	Product-Market-Dominance	Stack-Market-Dominance
Best Practices	Lean Startup	Scaling Silicon Valley Style	MBA Curriculum
Shareholder value	Future Opportunity	Sales Growth	Profit Growth

ROLAND: Not at all. As you can see in table 1.1, we are showing a third way: the scaleup way. Too many scaleup teams battle over remaining "startuppy" versus acting "professionally" (read "corporate"). Our book is showing that *neither* is right. The most appropriate prescriptions are *specific to the scaleup stage*. Neither startup ways nor corporate ways would help scaleups succeed here.

DOUG: Then how exactly do you define a scaleup company?

ROLAND: A scaleup is a growth company beyond product-market-fit, looking for product-market-dominance. As such it is not a startup, a growth company before product-market-fit. Nor is it an incumbent (also known as a steady corporation, a mature business, a going concern company or a "stay-up").

DOUG: So it is an in-between kind of company?

ROLAND: Exactly. It is a different animal from a startup, and also a different animal from an incumbent. In striving towards product-market-dominance, it has its own unique purpose. It also has its own typical challenges and its own management prescriptions. Its own best practices, if you will. All these are different from both a startup and an incumbent.

1.2   Who: Founders of Tech Scaleups

DOUG: Whom would you say we wrote the book for?

ROLAND: We especially want to reach the founders of tech scaleups. Those in charge of a startup that has "hit it" and is struggling to serve surging demand for their product. Which means the founders are struggling too. To hire enough people, to align the teams and to raise enough funds for the next stage.

> *"Let us be honest. Scaleup success depends*
> *completely on the founders"*
>
> ROLAND SIEBELINK

DOUG: Is there a reason to target founders? Why not any scaleup leader, executive or even employee?

ROLAND: Of course, all these people are welcome to read our book and I am sure they will find much valuable advice. But to be completely honest: the degree of scaleup success still depends completely on the founders.

- It is founders who are leading the growth company through successive scaleup stages.

- It is founders, more than anyone else, who need to change their behavior as the company grows.

- And it is founders who are most at risk of losing their job if the company fails to succeed in the next scaleup stage.

DOUG: We are talking in particular about founders of tech companies? Ventures that have attracted outside investments from angels or venture capitalists?

ROLAND: Yes, the tech industry is a particular focus of this book. Of course, many of our prescriptions have helped growth companies around the world. Whether they be in construction, hospitality, business-to-business-services, you name it.

> *"In tech, the winner-takes-all model explains*
> *why seeking outside funding makes most sense"*

ROLAND SIEBELINK

But what none of these industries have in common with tech is the ability to conquer an entire market. This winner-takes-all-model is what makes the payoff of investing in technology so great.

- It explains why the predominant business model for tech is to seek outside funding.

- It drives the much faster growth rates that the tech industry is famous for.

- And it clarifies why founders of tech companies need to learn fast if they are to keep their CEO position.

1.3 Challenge: Continued High Failure Rate

DOUG: Once a startup reaches product-market-fit, investors must be lining up?

ROLAND: You are right, raising money becomes easier at that stage. The risk is much lower when there is sustainable traction, with first revenues earned.

DOUG: Then it must be all smooth sailing from there. Once you have a proven business model, investments will flow in and you can enjoy the ride.

ROLAND: It is not so simple. Startup literature gives the impression that, after product-market-fit, it is *all* smooth sailing. That is not a reflection of reality, but of most startup advisers' focus on the early-stage.

The truth is that, after product-market-fit, new "hard things" keep emerging (Horowitz, 2014). Few people realize that scaleups still fail often after several rounds of financing (see figure 1.1). It is not a smooth ride. Quite the opposite. That is the reason we wanted to make this book available to founders. Founders face new challenges at every new stage and many of them fail to adapt. I call it the Silicon Valley roller coaster.

DOUG: Meaning that founders can expect lots of ups and downs?

ROLAND: Lots of ups and downs. And feeling pulled in completely unexpected directions. And getting nauseous. And fearing for your life. All that, exactly like a real rollercoaster. But without the guardrails.

DOUG: Once a startup reaches product-market-fit, will it always become a successful scaleup?

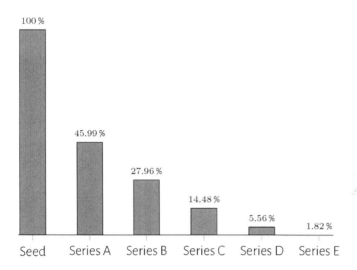

Figure 1.1: Tech Scaleups—Fundraising Success Rates by Stage

ROLAND: Not at all. At each funding stage, on average 54% of scaleups never raise a subsequent round (CB Insights, 2017). So across the four funding rounds we cover in these two books (from seed funding through series E), you are looking at a 2% survival rate. And this is of all the startups that were able to raise a seed round. If we include those that did not, the survival rate would be far lower.

DOUG: Not raising a next round is not necessarily a failure, though.

ROLAND: True, many of the companies drop off the chart because they exit. Sometimes for substantial money—sometimes for less than investors put it. I just simplified the chart because I compare it to the trajectory most founders strive for in their tech startup. All the way to Series E and an IPO.

1.4 Assumption: Automatic Growth

DOUG: What causes this high failure rate?

ROLAND: At a superficial level, it is almost always that the scaleup did not meet its growth targets.

DOUG: Right, it is all about growing the company.

ROLAND: Growth is the part all founders and investors can agree on. But growth is a result, a lagging metric. Unless you assume that growth will be automatic, the question is how to reach and sustain that growth.

DOUG: How *do* scaleups reach and sustain that growth?

ROLAND: Well, founders asking themselves that question would already be a start. It would make the team aware that product-market-fit is only the beginning of the journey. That it requires hard work to sustain the growth founders have projected to investors. On top of that, the kind of work starts changing and it requires new competences and behaviors. Behaviors often at odds to what worked well when the founders were still leading a startup.

"Even after product-market-fit,
growth does not come automatically"

ROLAND SIEBELINK

DOUG: We would caution against assuming growth is automatic.

ROLAND: Absolutely. The notion that growth is automatic may seem ludicrous to some. But unfortunately, many startup founders do share that assumption. Startup manuals have trained founders to see product-market-fit as the ultimate goal. *Once you reach product-market-fit, you have made it as a founder. You have more customers than you can handle. Investors will line up. Eternal glory will be yours.* In other words, automatic.

DOUG: With that expectation, scaleup teams are bound to miss their growth projections.

ROLAND: Indeed. Teams are surfing a wave of market demands and fool themselves it will last forever. Targets get set too high, the company cannot find enough sales people in time, investors lose fate. But there are other root causes causing these slumps in growth.

1.5 Problem: Missing Playbook

DOUG: What are these underlying causes? What can founders do to avoid this fate of failure?

ROLAND: I am tempted to name many causes. Undisciplined growth, founder strife, losing focus, etc. I could name ten more. But for me, they all come together into one big challenge. That this is a difficult journey without a roadmap, a manual, a playbook for this stage (Blank, 2015).

DOUG: Why do you feel that playbook is so important?

ROLAND: Because businesses succeed to a large extent through alignment. Playbooks provide that very alignment, especially in fast-changing

"I wish someone had a methodology as simple as The Lean Startup for how to scale my company"

"PATRICK" QUOTED BY STEVE BLANK

circumstances. The stronger the playbook, the less people will panic and the more they stay focused on the same goals.

DOUG: *Lean Startup* is a great example. It has helped so many tech founders align around common goals, learn new competences and know what to focus on.

ROLAND: Yes, you can consider it the bible for tech *startups*. But for tech scaleups, no such playbook has existed. Every founder and employee must figure out for themselves what to do.

The little existing advice out there from Reid Hoffman (2017b), Yeh and McCann (2015) and Andreessen Horowitz (2014) is not bad but feels rather anecdotal. There is no clear path or process to follow as there was with *Lean Startup*.

DOUG: So how do founding teams reach agreement on what to do?

ROLAND: The truth is that they often fail to. As long as things keep going well, it is easy to keep the spirits up. But as soon as growth hits the inevitable snag, the fact that there is no common playbook starts to hurt.

Without a clear roadmap to follow, each founder and board member has different ideas on what to do. Soon it seems as if the only possible compromise is to try a bit of everything. The company loses focus, starts squandering resources, loses belief and momentum. Any scaleup finds it hard to recover from that.

Figure 1.2: Startup Tools No Longer Helpful for Scaleups

DOUG: This is why we felt so compelled to write this book for founders...

ROLAND: Indeed, to provide that playbook and save scaleups from disaster.

DOUG: What does this journey without a roadmap imply for founders?

ROLAND: Founders experience different scaleup phases exactly like a roller coaster. They brace themselves for some new challenge, and impact they expect. Yet they find themselves pulled in a completely different and unexpected direction.

Founders find that unexpected pull is the defining characteristic of the scaleup phase. That they were doing fine in the last level of the game. But at this new level, the rules have changed. And then changed again for the level after that.

Leaders of these growth companies need to learn a tremendous amount in almost no time. Very few are able to adapt and keep an aura of credible leadership. All the way from raising their series A to their series D.

DOUG: Then, what happens? Do founders resign or does the company fail or do they learn to cope?

> *"Four out of five entrepreneurs [are] forced*
> *to step down from the CEO's post"*

NOAM WASSERMAN

ROLAND: It is a Silicon Valley tragedy that investors often force a leadership change. All venture capitalists start of founder-friendly, investing in teams, coaching the founders, et cetera. Yet the standard VC playbook long included a CEO replacement. It was often a condition for raising series B, or at the latest series C.

DOUG: This was all planned as part of the investment?

ROLAND: Absolutely. Conventional wisdom held that founders could "choose between being rich or being royal" (Wasserman, 2008). They could either keep control, or allow professional management to take over. Only professional management would build the company into something valuable. The choice was not always a real one. Wasserman (2008) found that "Four out of five entrepreneurs [were] forced to step down from the CEO's post."

1.6 Desire: Lead a Successful IPO

DOUG: Where do founders want to get to, after they have reached product-market-fit?

ROLAND: Most founders focus on successive funding rounds. They try to keep growing the company all the way to Unicorn status and/or an IPO.

DOUG: Making these founders incredibly rich.

ROLAND: That is what the press would have you believe. And indeed, some of the most successful founders have made billions of dollars. But the press ignores the many founders focused too much on raising ever more capital. So much that they had diluted their holding to almost nothing.

DOUG: They would still make a few million bucks on exit.

ROLAND: Of course, and a few million is nothing to sneer at. My point is that they might have kept more of the company with a different goal in mind. If they had focused on maximizing their market power, rather than capital raised.

DOUG: Just like a startup should focus more on the milestone of product-market-fit than on raising seed funding?

ROLAND: Yes, that is a very good comparison. And the new milestone should be to turn the product-market-fit into product-market-dominance.

DOUG: Why product-market-dominance?

ROLAND: Because it attacks the most common causes of scaleup failure. Let me illustrate with the help of Jason Calacanis, who identified three common reasons why (funded) startups fail *after* product-market-fit: (Calacanis, 2017)

1. "When the market does not show the scale, velocity or depth to sustain initial margins;

2. "When there are too many competitors in the market, competing each other to death;

3. "When founders get emboldened and move to the next thing too early."

DOUG: Is there a common theme between these three reasons?

ROLAND: I think there is. I think it is the failure to turn product-market-fit into product-market-dominance.

With product-market-fit, the startup secures a main foothold in a market. But when can they turn that foothold into unassailable market leadership? So that the company and investors can reap the benefits of the superior offering.

Each of the reasons above represents a failure to reach product-market-dominance in time.

DOUG: Can you show us the link between the above reasons and product-market-dominance?

ROLAND: Of course! Let us take them one by one:

Scale reasons This sounds like an intrinsic market problem. But often it points to a failure to scale into and dominate the *entire market*. Beyond the early adopters.

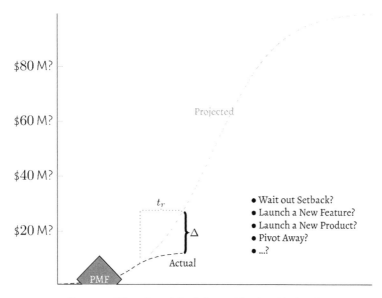

Figure 1.3: When Growth Stalls Beyond Product-Market-Fit

Competition reasons Failure to protect the unique product-market-fit with barriers to entry.

Distraction reasons Failure to stick with the product-market penetration. At least until early majority leadership is within reach.

Setting product-market-dominance as the key goal post product-market-fit is crucial in tech companies. The marginal cost of advanced technology development is low to non-existent. So, as table 1.2 shows, tech markets converge onto one gorilla that completely dominates the category.

DOUG: You must become the gorilla in your market.

Table 1.2: Many Examples of Winner-Takes-All-Markets in Tech

Industry	"Took-all"-winner
PC Software	Microsoft
Enterprise databases	Oracle
Search engines	Google
Social media	Facebook
E-commerce	Amazon
CRM software	SalesForce.com
HR software	Workday
ERM software	SAP
Company chat	Slack
Etc, etc, etc	Etc, etc, etc

ROLAND: That is exactly my point. Once a startup reaches product-market-fit, it shows potential to both investors and competitors. It is crucial to focus all energy and resources on securing market leadership. Otherwise the startup will condemn itself to also-ran status.

In other words, as soon as you reach product-market-fit, the game changes. Startups that adopt the scaleup playbook have a good chance of becoming the gorilla. Those that stick with the startup playbook for too long must fail. Even after reaching product-market-fit.

DOUG: I am not sure I have heard this term "product-market-dominance" before. Where does it come from and what does it mean?

ROLAND: *Product-market-dominance* means having an unassailable leadership position in your product-market. It means:

1. having the biggest market share in the product-market

2. enjoying majority recognition as the #1 in the product-market

3. having established an impregnable "moat" around your "castle" (Hargreaves, 2017).

DOUG: Why did you introduce a new term?

ROLAND: I noticed scaleup founders focused too much on product-market-*fit*. So I started using product-market-*dominance* as a counter-weight.

By the mid 2010s, the term product-market-*fit* was well established. *Lean Startup* made founders great at iterating through build-measure-learn cycles. Reaching product-market-fit seemed to be all that mattered.

One day, I started noticing a dangerous pattern in my talks with scaleup leaders. As soon as they reached product-market-fit, they started working on a second product. And a third. As if their only purpose was to develop new products.

DOUG: They abandoned the product as soon as it "fit" the market?

ROLAND: Not quite "abandoned," more like "left to its own devices." As if product-market-fit represented the end point of the founder's purpose. As if the milestone of product-market-fit meant a job completed.

DOUG: Have they not? I thought all startup literature suggested that product-market-fit is the goal?

ROLAND: And it is. For the startup phase. But it is not because the business has overcome the startup phase, that its journey has ended. It has simply turned into a different kind of company: a scaleup.

DOUG: And rather than for product-market-fit, it should aim for product-market-dominance?

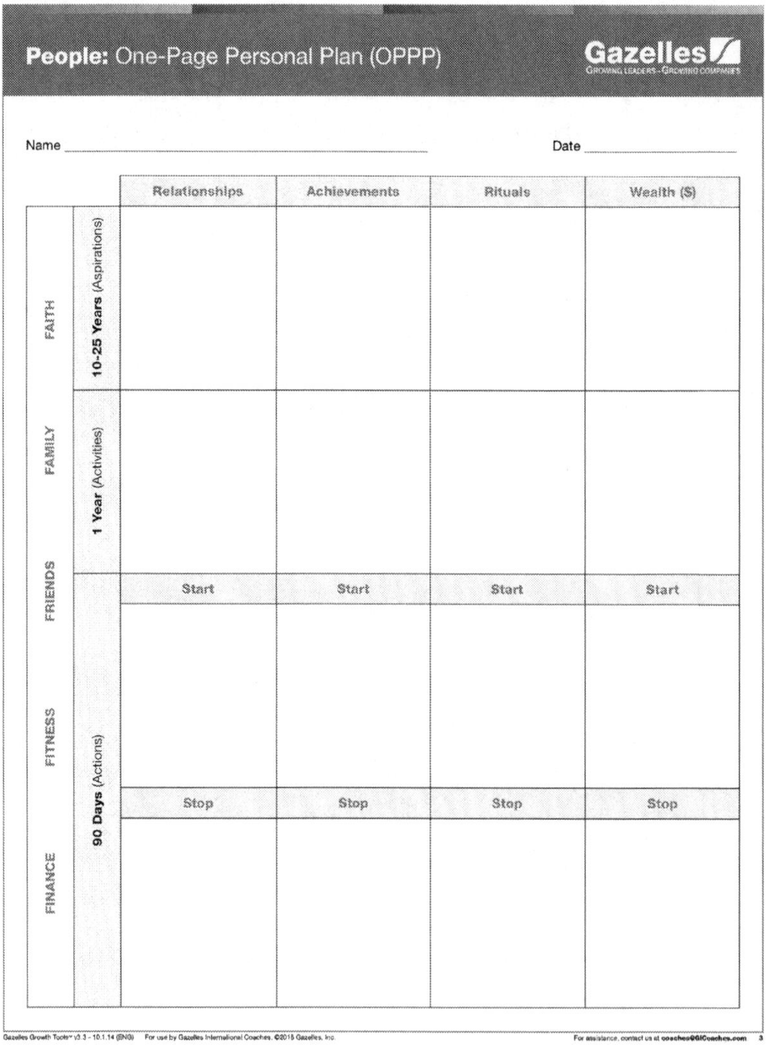

People: One-Page Personal Plan (OPPP)

Gazelles
GROWING LEADERS - GROWING COMPANIES

Name ______________________ Date ____________

		Relationships	Achievements	Rituals	Wealth ($)
FAITH	**10-25 Years** (Aspirations)				
FAMILY	**1 Year** (Activities)				
FRIENDS	**90 Days** (Actions)	Start	Start	Start	Start
FITNESS					
		Stop	Stop	Stop	Stop
FINANCE					

Gazelles Growth Tools™ v3.3 - 10.1.14 (ENG) For use by Gazelles International Coaches. ©2015 Gazelles, Inc. For assistance, contact us at **coaches@GICoaches.com** 3

Figure 1.4: Gazelles OPPP: Founders, What Do You Want?

ROLAND: Exactly! The main job of the scaleup is to reach product-market-dominance. To reach the #1 position in the product-market they have found. Before incumbents can block their ascent.

DOUG: I guess most founders would rather develop new products than enter that battle.

ROLAND: Exactly, many feel more comfortable sticking to what they know and where they have reached success. But the business needs a leader willing to scale. That leader does not have to be the founder, though it is of great advantage if it is.

DOUG: How do you figure out if the founder is still in the right place, leading the company?

ROLAND: What matters is that the purpose of the leader is aligned to the scaling phase the company needs. I often ask founders to draw up their One Page Personal Plan (see figure 1.4) to discover their own purpose—and whether it is aligned to that of the company.

1.7 How: Following the Scaleup Roadmap

DOUG: So the challenge is to overcome a landscape of obstacles and high failure rates. To lead your startup to a successful IPO. In other words, it needs to become more like a big corporation.

ROLAND: Wrong. This is another reason we wrote this book. To fight against the tendency to copy big corporations too early. Too many teams that accept that they can no longer act like a startup, try and start to act like a mature company or an incumbent. I find this causes as much damage as sticking with the startup script for too long.

DOUG: Really? Is that not the goal of a scaleup company? To grow up?

ROLAND: It is, but not all at once. I reject the binary distinction of a startup versus an incumbent or mature company. Growing up is a trajectory. Who wants a college kid to behave like a 45-year-old before they have even graduated? Growth companies need to go through different phases. Like kids and young adults do.

DOUG: People think about startups and mature corporations in too binary a way.

ROLAND: And it causes strife! Founders want to keep alive the startup spirit. But new executives want things to "turn professional." Next thing you know, there are consultants and fat PowerPoint decks. Tons of licenses for software that does not talk to each other. And reams of irrelevant process documentation.

DOUG: "Professionals" who come from mature incumbents feel their habits are the only way to run a company.

ROLAND: But they forget that a scaleup's main goal is not risk reduction, but product-market-dominance. Let alone that it has no budget to deal with "professional best practices."

DOUG: It sounds like a big internal fight.

ROLAND: That is exactly right. Many scaleups are in constant battle between "startup people" and "professionals." But what should their battle be about?

DOUG: About reaching product-market-dominance! A battle against the competition!

Figure 1.5: From Product-Market-Fit to Product-Market-Dominance

> *"Scaleups should not focus on risk reduction*
> *but on reaching product-market-dominance"*

ROLAND SIEBELINK

ROLAND: Indeed. At best, the fights between "startup people" and "professionals" lead to compromise. At worst, they lead to a complete lack of focus on what the company needs to achieve. Rigid corporate processes create bureaucracy where the scaleup needs to stay agile. Hyperspecialization creates huge bottlenecks in responsiveness where the scaleup needs to remain "cool."

DOUG: So what is the alternative?

ROLAND: It is the model we describe in this book. That there are three main stages rather than two:

1. The startup stage—before product-market-fit

2. The scaleup stage—between product-market-fit and product-market-dominance

3. The mature stage—post product-market-dominance

In the next few chapters, we will start outlining the scaleup stage in full detail, from the freshman phase to the senior phase.

1.8   A Book in Two Volumes

DOUG: We decided to describe the scaleup roadmap in two volumes.

ROLAND: Yes, this book is Volume I. It contains the mid-stage journey from applicant scaleups to sophomore scaleups. Or from Seed funding to series C. Our next book will be Volume II, talking about the late-stage journey from Series C through Exit. Or Unicorn status. Or IPO.

DOUG: For our audience, can you share the reason behind this split?

ROLAND: Yes, absolutely. As we were presenting the content of the scaleup rollercoaster in events around the world, our events almost always led to a focus either on the mid-stage or on the late-stage challenges. Relatively few people wanted to delve into detail around both. So it seemed to make sense to make the knowledge available in two separate volumes. That way we could allow ourselves to go deeper in each volume.

DOUG: And as we write this in Q1/2018, when are we planning to have both books available?

ROLAND: As of our writing this, this volume I is scheduled to be available for preorder in March 2018 and to be fully published in April 2018. Volume II should be available for preorder in Q1/2019 and then be fully published in Q2/2019.

DOUG: What if people are particularly interested in the late stage scaleup roadmap before our book comes out?

ROLAND: We will start publishing some draft excerpts on our blog (www.scaleupallies.com) starting in Q3/2018. And of course we are always happy to come do a lunch-and-learn at tech scaleups with content customized for their specific situation.

Roadmap: the Scaleup Roller Coaster

2.1 Defining a Scaleup

DOUG: We have introduced the concept of a scaleup now. How exactly is a scaleup different from a startup?

ROLAND: That is simple. A startup is a venture that is still looking for product-market-fit. A scaleup has already found product-market-fit and is looking for product-market-dominance.

DOUG: I'm confused, what about Lyft, Dropbox, AirBnB, Spotify? All these famous startups that have long "hit it" and are growing like crazy? Do you not call them startups?

ROLAND: No, I would call them scaleups. Lyft and Dropbox, at the time of writing, have not reached product-market-dominance. Spotify is close and AirBnB arguably has reached product-market-dominance, so I would call them incumbents by now.

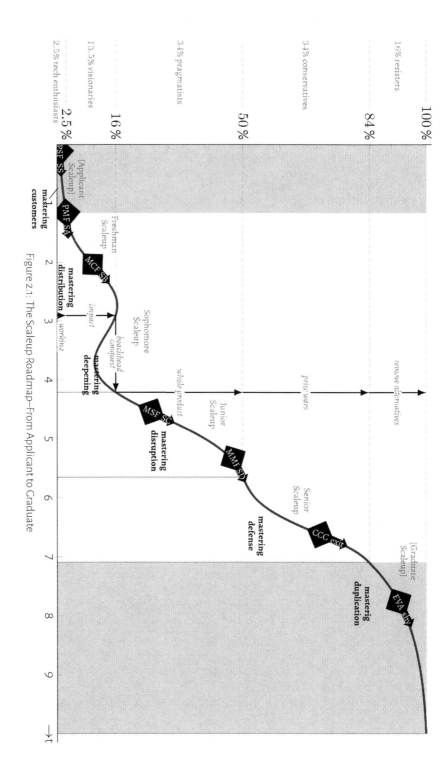

Figure 2.1: The Scaleup Roadmap—From Applicant to Graduate

*"A scaleup is a former startup
that has 'hit' product-market-fit"*

ROLAND SIEBELINK

DOUG: How does our definition differ from how other people use the word "startup"?

ROLAND: The classic Silicon Valley definition of a startup is: any venture-funded company *pre-exit*. Meaning that the company has not sold itself or launched an IPO. I find this definition not incorrect, but problematic in guiding founders.

First, it puts disparate development stages of a company into one "startup" bucket. Second, the pre-exit stage is much longer than it used to be. That compounds the first problem.

DOUG: What is the problem with putting disparate development stages of a company into one "startup" bucket?

ROLAND: Many founders infer from this a black-and-white thinking on how to manage companies. "The Startup Way" pre-exit and "the Traditional Way" post-exit.

DOUG: Why is that so problematic?

ROLAND: Because this confusion causes more founders and growth companies to fail. There is a vast difference between:

- leading a *startup, pre* product-market-fit

- leading a *scaleup, post* product-market-fit.

55

One is a small team looking for a match between their product ideas and a market. The other is a large team racing towards dominance of their market with a proven product.

My point is that each stage has its own recipes for success. If founders are not conscious of how demands on them change with scale, they will fail. What worked for them in one stage will damage their results in the next stage.

DOUG: Can you give us an example?

ROLAND: This book is full of examples, of course! But I can highlight a common situation. Successful early startups have a stubborn hands-on founder. They delight early customers with detailed command of the customer experience.

In scaleups, founders who remain hands-on become bottlenecks. (Wickman, 2013) Their need to decide everything blocks the growth of the organization. This is a common cause for scaleup implosion.

> *"It's not practical for you to remain*
> *chef, head waiter, and dishwasher*
> *as your company grows."*
>
> GINO WICKMAN

2.2   Comparing Ventures to Kids

DOUG: Back to how to define a startup, broad or narrow. You made an interesting analogy with raising kids.

ROLAND: Yes, for venture capitalists, all their portfolio companies are like kids. Kids are their parents' financial responsibility until they have "left the nest." Toddlers, school kids, teens and college kids, the same broad financial definition applies. Financially, they are all kids until they earn their own keep. The same for growth companies: they are all "startups" in the sense that they have not exited yet.

DOUG: Yet how you raise a toddler better be very different from how you raise a teen.

ROLAND: Exactly my point. From an advisory and education perspective, a single "kid" definition is too broad. Each stage of development requires its own skills. What helps a toddler get ahead is completely different from what makes a teen successful. A toddler crawling, singing aloud, saying whatever they think is very cute. A teenager, not so much. Every stage has a new set of success criteria, and requires new competences to fulfill them.

> *"What made you cool as a startup*
> *will not make you cool as a scaleup,*
> *and what made you attractive as a scaleup*
> *will not make you attractive as an incumbent."*

ROLAND SIEBELINK

DOUG: And you see the same phenomenon with growth companies?

ROLAND: The very same phenomenon indeed. An early-stage startup needs hands-on founders, a hacking mindset and constant pivoting. A late-stage scaleup will implode if it follows those prescriptions. Instead, it needs clockmaker founders (Collins, 2001), intense market focus and rapid issue resolution. And once it turns into a mature corporation, it will need yet different prescriptions.

DOUG: The success criteria change as you scale.

ROLAND: Yes, that is the very essence of what this book is about. How founders can learn to ride that rollercoaster while staying in charge. While staying a good parent to their growing scaleup, if you will. (Harnish, 2002)

DOUG: Thanks, that is crystal-clear. But on page 55, you mentioned a second reason against defining startups as "any venture pre-exit." Why else is this not helpful?

ROLAND: Correct. These days, ventures can stay out of public markets much longer than they used to. The rule was to go public when reaching $100M in revenues.

Nowadays, many growth companies prefer to keep scaling in private. They can do so because more private investors are eager to invest. But also because of secondary markets. These have allowed insiders to realize some of their wealth without a listing.

This compounds the problem we mentioned above. We now have "startups" making billions in revenues and employing 10,000s of people. In such companies, classic startup advice like "move fast and break things" is no longer helpful. Calling any company pre-exit a "startup" becomes meaningless.

DOUG: If "startup" is such a broad term, then what do you prefer?

"A late-stage scaleup will implode
if it follows the prescriptions for an early startup"

ROLAND SIEBELINK

ROLAND: I prefer startup—scaleup—incumbent. In this lineup I define a startup narrowly with Blank (2005) and Ries (2011). A startup is a company still seeking a replicable, scalable business model. In other words, one that has not yet found product-market-fit.

DOUG: So what happens when a startup reaches that famous product-market-fit?

ROLAND: Then it ceases to be a startup. But at the same time, they are nowhere near incumbent status. That is why we need a new term: scaleup. A growth company beyond product-market-fit, but before the product-market-dominance that characterizes incumbents.

DOUG: So every growth company is first a startup, then a scaleup, then an incumbent?

ROLAND: Those that succeed and survive, yes. Unfortunately, most growth companies stumble on the trajectory to becoming an incumbent. Especially in the scaleup stage. That is why we wrote this book.

DOUG: To serve as guidance for scaleup leaders.

ROLAND: Exactly. Our book helps guide founders of scaleup companies along the rollercoaster journey. From Series A through Series D. And from initial product-market-fit, all the way to ultimate product-market-dominance.

2.3 Comparing the Scaleup Journey to College

DOUG: Sticking with the analogy to raising kids, this would mean scale-ups are like college students.

ROLAND: Exactly! Still dependent for finances on their parents or investors. But finding their identity and strengths and learning to stand on their own feet.

DOUG: This scaleup phase seems quite a journey. How many years do you expect it to last?

ROLAND: Between four and seven years from reaching product-market-fit. Like a full college education in most countries.

Having said that, I do not like to time box the scaleup phase. Because it is less about the time spent and more about the competences built up. That is why I also like that college analogy. To use the US college terminology, from freshman through sophomore through junior to senior scaleup. A program you can study and then graduate.

DOUG: I have noticed these terms are a bit US-centric, how do other countries refer to this journey?

ROLAND: In other countries we might call this from first-year through second-year through third-year to fourth-year scaleup. I did not want to imply that every phase takes exactly one year, so I decided to stick with the US terminology.

It still has the connotation of four years, of course. But it also invokes a journey from childhood dependence to full adulthood. As well as all the new skills that you learn while you are at college:

1. Freshman scaleups

2. Sophomore scaleups

3. Junior scaleups

4. Senior scaleups

DOUG: Then where in this college model would you place startups and incumbents ?

ROLAND: We can stretch the analogy with pre-college and the post-college phases. A startup is like a scaleup applicant, an incumbent is like a scaleup graduate. These are the terms we have used to label this book's chapters.

DOUG: Tell me why you use these college terms. Why not talk about a Series A funded company, a Series B funded company etc?

ROLAND: Because the funding that a company has may be out of whack with its level of maturity. The funding does not always match the archetype of the situation they find themselves in.

Some scaleups reach junior level before raising Series A. Some may never even raise external capital at all.

DOUG: Can the opposite happen too? Raising money earlier than our model would predict?

ROLAND: It is rarer, but it happens. I should think of new startups by founders with a successful previous exit. They tend to raise a big Series A before even finding problem-solution-fit.

DOUG: So the amount raised or the order of the Series is not always a good sign for how far the scaleup has matured.

Table 2.1: The Scaleup Roadmap Across Multiple Dimensions of Maturity

	Startup (Applicant Scaleup)	Freshman Scaleup	Sophomore Scaleup	Junior Scaleup	Senior Scaleup	Incumbent (Graduate Scaleup)
Customer served	Technology Enthusiasts	Visionary business users	Mainstream Beachhead	Early Majority	Late Majority	Laggards
Milestone reached	Problem-solution-fit	Product-market-fit	Market-channel-fit	Main-stream fit	Multiseg-ment fit	Market Dominance
Funds raised	Seed	Series A	Series B	Series C	Series D	Exit/Unicorn
Product status	Functioning	Impactful	Solving	Crushing	Dominat-ing	Conserving
Mastering	Serving	Distribution	Deepening	Disrupt-ing	Defending	Duplicating
Employees est.	3..8	9..26	27..80	81..242	243..728	729..2186
Revenue est. MUSD	0-1	1-5	5-25	25-100	100-500M	$500-

ROLAND: That is exactly it. This is why we prefer to label our stages with neutral terms like freshman and sophomore. That way, they can contain many more dimensions of maturity.

2.4 Not Just About Raising Money

DOUG: So what changes in the various financing rounds? Once you have raised money once, do you not get better at it every time you try again?

ROLAND: You may be right in that founders get more comfortable with raising money. But your question also betrays a syndrome that many tech founders fall victim to. A planning driven by fundraising needs.

DOUG: What do you mean? Is raising money not the key job for tech founders?

ROLAND: Raising money is a responsibility of the founders. Several rounds prove the success of the company in the eyes of investors. But people forget that funds add no fundamental value to the market power.

New funds raised help prove that the fundamentals of the company have improved. Especially when the new funds come in at a higher valuation than the previous round. But they do not in themselves improve business fundamentals. Other than short-term cash flow flexibility.

DOUG: Of course! The fundamentals must be product-solution-fit, product-market-fit, initial revenues and so on?

ROLAND: Even these are outcomes of basic processes that I often guide founders to. The best practices that I would like them to learn. For example: product-solution-fit is the outcome of a disciplined iteration process. It includes:

1. setting clear hypotheses;

2. leaving your building to talk to customers

3. validating hypotheses

4. turning hypotheses into learning;

5. starting the cycle all over again.

It is not enough to command a team to reach product-solution-fit. To actually deliver product-solution-fit, founders need to design and lead the process. They need to set the right example and instill the discipline. They need to live the the scientific method that underpins this method.

The same goes for follow-up outcomes that investors want to see. Founders cannot tell their team to prepare for series B. They need to explain what Series B requires. But they also need to get their hands dirty in setting up sales and marketing. Let alone set the right parameters for what people the company will hire and promote.

DOUG: It is not only about raising money.

ROLAND: Exactly. It is about building up new competences in the organization. Competences that will lead to new and coveted outcomes. It is those outcomes that will help raise money at an improved valuation.

Founders who only focus on the fundraising journey will set up their company for failure. Founders who build the right competences in the organization, will reap the rewards. They will find investors lining up to offer their funds, rather than having to go and ask for investments.

2.5   The Scaleup Roadmap

DOUG: This book then represents an entire roadmap throughout that scaleup journey. From series A to Series D.

ROLAND: Or, as I would prefer to call it, from applicant to graduate scaleup. An entire roadmap along the most telling dimensions of maturity:

- Type of customer served

- Milestone reached

- Funds raised

- Product status

- Competence mastering

- Number of employees

- Revenue estimate

DOUG: Can we get a bit more context? For example, what do you mean with "type of customer served"?

ROLAND: This indicates where the scaleups' customers are in the technology adoption curve. From technology enthusiasts through laggards (Linowes, 1999).

DOUG: What about "milestone reached"?

65

ROLAND: What "fit" has the scaleup already achieved. Starting with problem-solution-fit, our famous product-market-fit, all the way through product-market-dominance.

DOUG: "Funds raised" should be self-explanatory.

ROLAND: Yes but we are more interested in how many rounds they have closed than in the actual amounts. This an estimate of what "series" that funding represented. The few tech scaleups that have funded their growth with internal cash flow can ignore this line.

DOUG: What do you mean with "product status"?

ROLAND: I am talking about the level of maturity of the product, and the degree of market acceptance. Is the core technology barely functional (demo stage)? Or is the product already disrupting/crushing a previous solution?

DOUG: Does "mastering" represent the next "bump" on the roller coaster?

ROLAND: Exactly! It is key competence the scaleup team needs to make their own, above all other priorities, to make the next level.

DOUG: And then there are size estimates of the workforce and the revenues.

ROLAND: Yes, we include a very rough estimate of how many employees the scaleup has by this stage. We see much variation here so please use this as an indicator only.

DOUG: Same goes for the revenues?

ROLAND: Yes, this is another estimate for those that want a benchmark. Of course, revenues are dependent on the industry, the vertical and the product. So please thread even more lightly with these numbers.

DOUG: Thank you for taking us through all those dimensions. But, does it not feel too structured? People will say that every company is different. Funding can come earlier or later than in our model. But the same goes for the customer targeted or for when competition appears. All can come earlier or later than we predict.

ROLAND: Of course, every scaleup is different. Individual factors may combine in a different way than in our model. All we are doing is to outline the most common scenario. So that founders can compare their own venture against the model. And understand where their own experience is deviating.

> *"Any intelligent fool can make*
> *things bigger and more complex...*
> *It takes a touch of genius—and a lot of courage—*
> *to move in the opposite direction."*

> E. F. SCHUMACHER

2.6 Applicant Scaleups: Mastering Customers

DOUG: Applicant scaleups are really startups, is that not right?

ROLAND: Yes, correct, they are startups in the classic sense, companies before product-market-fit. They hope to transition to the first scaleup stage.

DOUG: What are the typical characteristics of these Applicant scaleups?

ROLAND: If I may be so blunt, most startups at this stage scream "early stage" across most of our dimensions.

DOUG: What does that mean for the type of customer they sell to?

ROLAND: The few paying customers that applicant scaleups have are technology enthusiasts/innovators. People who love the technology for its own sake and for its potential. Who love to tinker with it themselves but who do not look to make business impact with it yet.

DOUG: These are still companies before product-market-fit, right? Have they reached a different milestone?

ROLAND: Yes, proper applicant scaleups *have* reached problem-solution-fit. The founders are no longer shopping around a solution looking for a problem. Applicant scaleups have gone through enough *build-measure-learn* cycles. They have matched their technology to a real problem that customers want solved. Startups need to have reached this stage before I accept them as scaleup applicants.

DOUG: Have they raised funding already?

ROLAND: Yes, I would expect applicant scaleups to have raised a seed round from angel investors.

DOUG: How far along is their product at this early stage?

ROLAND: Applicant scaleups' products are functional. Demonstrating that "it works" is the core of the pitch.

DOUG: If the product is already working, what is the challenge they face?

ROLAND: Applicant scaleups are trying to master how to serve customers well. That means figuring out not only how to sign up customers and how to get paid. But also providing support, response to feature requests and solve bug reports.

DOUG: I assume their team is still small at this stage.

ROLAND: Correct, most applicant scaleups have the founders and a few employees and interns . I see the total team size below ten.

DOUG: Are applicant scaleups even in business already? I mean, have they started selling their product?

ROLAND: Just barely. Applicant scaleups have very little revenue or none at all. Definitely below a million USD per year. They typically have few customers and a significant share of the ones they have are in trial mode.

2.7 Freshman Scaleups: Mastering Distribution

DOUG: The freshman scaleup is the first "real" scaleup stage.

ROLAND: Yes, freshman scaleups have reached product-market-fit. They have moved out of classic startup territory and into solid scaleup territory.

DOUG: What customers do freshman scaleups have?

ROLAND: Freshman scaleups are starting to sign up more paying customers. The bulk of customers they sell to now are visionary business users. People who love the technology less for its own sake and more for the impact it can generate. Customers in this stage look to use the product to gain a competitive advantage.

DOUG: What milestone have they reached and how much have they raised?

ROLAND: Freshman scaleups have reached product-market-fit. That means that they have found a market willing to pay for their problem-solution-fit. They have a working revenue model. Freshman scaleups have raised a Series A round from "proper" venture capitalists.

DOUG: How mature can you expect their product to be?

ROLAND: Freshman scaleups' products are not only functional. They are impacting people's business or lives. Anecdotal case studies dominate their marketing. They all explain how the product gave visionary buyers an unfair advantage.

DOUG: What, especially, do freshman scaleups need to learn?

ROLAND: Freshman scaleup teams are trying to master building up distribution. They want reliable marketing and sales processes that go beyond mere growth hacking.

DOUG: How big are freshman scaleups, in your mind?

ROLAND: Freshman scaleups have more people than the typical startup, from 10–25 employees. They still feel like close-knit families. But you do see the first distinctions between "managers" and "frontline workers" appear.

Freshman scaleups also start to have a more solid revenue base, from one to five million dollars per year.

2.8   Sophomore Scaleups: Mastering Deepening

DOUG: Freshman scaleups were trying to master distribution. So sophomore scaleups must have reached a scalable sales process.

ROLAND: Yes, sophomore scaleups have figured out distribution. They are adding much sales capacity, funded by a healthy gross margin on their product. New customers have a higher projected lifetime value than it cost to sign them up. But moving their product into mainstream markets is not proving as easy.

DOUG: What customer type are sophomore scaleups selling to?

ROLAND: This is a key challenge. Sophomore scaleups are running out of early adopters to sell to. Even across all the verticals or segments they have been targeting. They are having trouble breaking into the mainstream market.

DOUG: What milestone have sophomore scaleups reached?

ROLAND: Sophomore scaleups have reached market-channel-fit. They have found at least one channel to sell to their market cost-effectively. They have a working distribution model.

DOUG: And how much money have they raised?

ROLAND: Sophomore scaleups have raised a Series B round from venture capitalists. This allows them to ramp up scaling distribution before incumbents can move in.

DOUG: How far have sophomore scaleups' products penetrated into the marketplace?

ROLAND: People recognize sophomore scaleups' products as a real solution for a market problem. Anecdotal case studies make place for rankings in analyst reports and market shares.

DOUG: What challenge do sophomore scaleups have to master?

ROLAND: Sophomore scaleups are trying to break into the mainstream of pragmatic, non-visionary customers. They do this by "deepening" their serving of a well-targeted mainstream beachhead market. With better understanding, market customization and a 100% product solution (Moore, 2013).

DOUG: How big are sophomore scaleups' work forces and revenues?

ROLAND: Sophomore scaleups have scaled their revenue to between $5M–$25M per year. They are growing their workforce fast, from 25 to 80 employees. Functional departments are growing into their own. We start seeing several management layers below the CEO.

2.9 Junior Scaleups: Mastering Disruption

DOUG: We will discuss junior scaleups at length in our next book. But let us have a quick preview here. We are talking about growth companies that have entered the mainstream market?

ROLAND: Indeed, junior scaleups have figured out a "whole product." For at least one beachhead segment in the mainstream market. Their product is so superior to the incumbent that the majority of customers is starting to sign up. As a result, they are conquering that beachhead by storm.

DOUG: Where are junior scaleups' customers on the adoption curve?

ROLAND: Junior scaleups sign up mostly early majority customers. Pragmatic buyers who want to avoid risky product decisions. But who, once they do buy a new product, want to commit to it for the long term.

Identifying key processes, the business system and core competences

Scale-up Ally △

Happy Customer

1. Derive the key process steps for value delivery

Process #1	Process #2	Process #3	Process #4	Process #5	Process #6

Key Activities

2. List the core segments

Segment #1

needs
- •
- •
- •

Segment #2

needs
- •
- •
- •

Segment #3

needs
- •
- •
- •

☐ insourced
☐ outsourced

☐ insourced
☐ outsourced

☐ insourced
☐ outsourced

☐ insourced
☐ outsourced

☐ insourced
☐ outsourced

☐ insourced
☐ outsourced

Source: IMD International MBA Program, Lausanne.

Figure 2.2: Worksheet: Business System/Core Competences

DOUG: What is the milestone that turns sophomore scaleups into junior scaleups reached?

ROLAND: Junior scaleups have reached mainstream fit. Their product is now providing a 100% solution for at least one niche of mainstream customers. A niche they can build on to expand to adjacent niches.

DOUG: How much money have they raised?

ROLAND: Junior scaleups have raised a Series C round from venture capitalists. This enables them to embed themselves even deeper in their niche of superiority.

DOUG: What about their product maturity?

ROLAND: Junior scaleups' products are becoming the reference solution for a mainstream market. For tech companies in particular, "market leadership" starts crowding out any particular benefit.

DOUG: All right, what is the next challenge for junior scaleups?

ROLAND: Junior scaleup teams need to master how to disrupt the mainstream market. Like in the board game *Risk*, they target conquering the entire board through conquering one territory (niche) at a time. For every mainstream niche, they expand their competences. They get vertical knowledge, partner with the correct ecosystem, et cetera. All so that they can serve as the leading provider.

DOUG: How many people do junior scaleups employ?

ROLAND: Junior scaleups have a workforce of 100s of employees. They are often spread across several locations. Tech companies will have expanded across the Atlantic. Functional departments are dominant, but they start realizing they need cross-functional teams too. Junior scaleups build more project teams, product councils and emerging business unit councils.

DOUG: And how big are their revenues?

ROLAND: Junior scaleups sell between $25M–$100M a year. This is close to the traditional revenues required for an IPO.

2.10 Senior Scaleups: Mastering Defense

DOUG: Continuing the preview of our next book, junior scaleups have already mastered disrupting. So what else do senior scaleups need to master?

ROLAND: Senior scaleups need to defend from attack the rapid gains that they have made in the junior stage. Junior scaleups build out the fortresses. Senior scaleups dig the moats.

DOUG: What customer type are senior scaleups selling most to?

ROLAND: Senior scaleups sign up customers further down the mainstream. They target late majority buyers who are conservative and price-sensitive. More often than not, you see price wars at this stage.

DOUG: What milestone must companies have reached to enter this stage?

ROLAND: Senior scaleups have reached multi-segment fit. They have expanded beyond their initial beachhead of mainstream customers. They now have enough pieces on the chessboard to aspire to lead the market at large.

DOUG: How much funding should we imagine senior scaleups have?

ROLAND: Senior scaleups have raised a Series D round from venture capitalists. This enables them to reinforce market leadership. Acquisitions of smaller competitors and suppliers become more prevalent at this stage.

DOUG: What is senior scaleups' product maturity?

ROLAND: Products have reached the #1 position for customers who hate to get left behind. Their market share may still be lower than the previous incumbent's. But they have been able to relegate that incumbent's image to "yesteryear's solution."

DOUG: What challenge do they need to master?

ROLAND: Senior scaleups need to master defense. How to ensure competitors cannot copy their business model without much investment.

Senior scaleups complement patents and other "hard" barriers with new barriers to entry. E.g. ecosystems, partnerships, large user bases and big data collections. that are impossible to replicate without high upfront investment.

DOUG: How many employees do you find in senior scaleups?

ROLAND: Senior scaleups are larger companies. They employ several hundreds to a thousand employees, across several offices worldwide. Organizations become too complex to manage through functional departments. Hence, senior scaleups tend to reorganize around in cross-functional business units.

DOUG: How much revenue are senior scaleups making?

ROLAND: Senior scaleups make between $100M and $500M in annual revenue. They are likely preparing to file for an IPO. Or they are able to attract enough late-stage investments to remain private as a unicorn.

2.11 Graduate Scaleups: Mastering Duplication

DOUG: Graduate scaleups are no longer really in the scaleup stage. They have graduated from it and are now incumbents.

ROLAND: That is right. When a scaleup has reached complete product-market-dominance, it is by definition an incumbent. We stop calling it a scaleup.

DOUG: What customers do graduate scaleups serve?

ROLAND: As market leaders, they serve customers all across the mainstream. Incumbents often focus on converting laggards. They are the only source of growth at this level of market maturity.

DOUG: What milestone have they reached and how much have they raised?

ROLAND: Graduate scaleups have reached product-market-dominance. The big long-term goal for any scaleup. That means their growth curve is starting to slow down. Most companies have launched an initial public offering before this stage. Or they have sold themselves to a large acquirer. Rare decacorns like Uber may continue to raise Series E, F, G, H and so on.

DOUG: What is the product status for graduate scaleups?

ROLAND: Graduate scaleups' products are very mature. They include lots of solutions for edge cases accumulated over the years. If they sell software, they have also gone through several generations of developers. People dare not touch much of the code and the value proposition. So any further innovation is largely at the surface or with side projects.

DOUG: What, if anything, do graduate scaleups still need to learn? After all, they have graduated...

ROLAND: They have graduated from scaleup university, yes. But to keep growing, they need to keep adding other areas of growth to their portfolio. I call this "mastering duplication."

DOUG: How big are graduate scaleups, in your mind?

ROLAND: Graduate scaleups employ thousands of people. They organize themselves in several autonomous business units that are autonomous. The corporate center focuses only on managing the portfolio of businesses:

- Acquiring key suppliers, competitors and future threats;

- Driving maximum synergies out of the diverse portfolio;

- Divesting businesses that are no longer key.

DOUG: Are we expecting graduate scaleups to make billions of dollars?

ROLAND: In revenue, yes. The lower limit is some $500M/year but I would expect that to still be growing fast. A real scaleup graduate makes at least $1B in revenue and there is no upper limit in our model.

Applicant Scaleups (Startups): Mastering Customers

DOUG: Following the college journey metaphor, this chapter is about applicant scaleups. That means, companies who are not yet scaleups themselves?

ROLAND: Correct, this chapter is about what it takes to become a scaleup. About the admission criteria, if you will. Call it a double check on whether your growth company is ready to become a scaleup.

DOUG: In the road map, we summarize that challenge as "mastering customers." What do you mean with that?

ROLAND: Think of it as a shortcut to "mastering delivering customer satisfaction." This phase is all about the startup learning to serve real customers and solve real problems. And getting customers to pay for that product and service.

DOUG: What aspects of "mastering customers" are most important?

ROLAND: This chapter will touch on four in particular. Each is a key component of the "mastering customers" challenge:

- Reaching problem-solution-fit

- Ensuring the product is a pain killer

- Selling to technology enthusiasts

- Establishing revenue traction

3.1 Applicant Scaleups: Overview

DOUG: What should I imagine the typical applicant scaleup looks like?

ROLAND: First, this company will still feel and think like a real startup. A small company, with five to ten employees. Usually, there are two or three founders. There are also a few engineers. Other roles (business development/sales, marketing/PR and support) have one generalist each. Founders themselves also perform staff responsibilities such as recruiting, finance and administration, drawing up contracts etc.

DOUG: If you have never been in such a startup, the way the team operates may feel strange.

ROLAND: Yes, it is very different from working in an incumbent. The team is close and feels like a household. (Yeh and McCann, 2015) The founders are like parents. They discuss everything among themselves and tell the other team members what to do. Non-founding team members are quite junior in comparison. Early twentysomethings in their first job

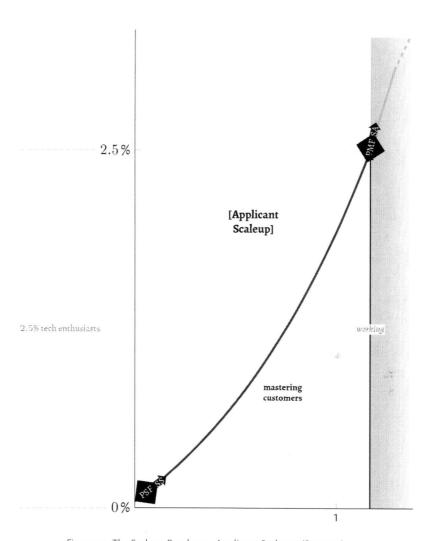

2.5 %

[**Applicant Scaleup**]

2.5% tech enthusiasts

working

mastering customers

PSF SS

PMF SA

0 %

1

Figure 3.1: The Scaleup Roadmap: Applicant Scaleups (Startups)

out of college. Or junior in their responsibilities. People who can execute assignments but could not replicate the founders' vision.

DOUG: Have they raised any money yet?

ROLAND: Yes, these startups have raised a seed round of between $500K and $1.5M, if based in Silicon Valley. Companies outside major venture hubs tend to raise a factor less for their seed round. Some companies raise this round only after they have established product-market-fit. Other startups may raise it on an unproven concept. Especially if (one of) the founder(s) has already made money for investors in a previous startup.

DOUG: Is their product still in the demoware stage?

ROLAND: No, they do have a working product, a "minimum value proposition." This product has gained initial traction in the marketplace. There are active users beyond friends and family, and there is some aspect of virality. Users are recommending the product to their friends and bringing in more users. This word-of-mouth implies *problem-solution-fit*. A "fit" between a customer problem and the solution the startup provides. The startup is enjoying growth without having to do active marketing.

> *"Many applicant startups avoid
> charging for their product"*
>
> ROLAND SIEBELINK

DOUG: How much are they selling at this stage?

ROLAND: Not much. The startup is essentially pre-revenue. Or revenues are negligible compared to the cash burn. The team has strong focus on optimizing product features. With which they can engage customers more and boost viral growth. Boosting sales is not yet the core focus. Many startups on purpose avoid charging for their product at this stage. Founders are well aware that pre-revenue companies attract different kinds of investors than post-revenue companies.

3.2 Recruited Household-Sized Team

DOUG: How big is the team of the startup at this stage?

ROLAND: We can call them household-sized, in line with the *Blitzscaling* course at Stanford (Yeh and McCann, 2015). That means that they will have between five and ten people, including the founders.

DOUG: That explains why they are still a startup, not yet a scaleup.

ROLAND: Well, to be exact, we do not distinguish a startup from a scaleup by size. But by whether they have already reached product-market-fit or not. But yes, you are right, most people would consider these companies classical startups.

DOUG: What does the team look like in this stage?

ROLAND: Of course, every applicant scaleup is different. But a typical configuration would include:

1. a Founder/CEO with business/product focus

2. a Founder/CTO with a technical/development focus

3. a few engineers, often in an offshore location

4. assuming they have started selling, one or two marketing/sales/ business development people

5. one administration/support/finance person who also does some recruiting.

DOUG: Why is the term "household" part of the blitzscaling lexicon?

ROLAND: According to Reid Hoffman, the term *household* implies more than size (Yeh and McCann, 2015). The team often works from an apartment or a garage, not from an office. They have lunch together, socialize together, and divide up the chores. Ordering lunch, getting basic office supplies, sometimes even clearing up the place.

It is hard to understate how much trust this early setting builds between early team members. They almost live together rather than just work together, often for for a few years.

DOUG: Are co-working spaces not popular with applicant scaleups too?

ROLAND: Absolutely, especially before the founders hire their first employee. Once a team starts growing beyond the founders, there is a need to build strong team spirit. The availability of some seed capital often leads an applicant scaleup to rent its own place. Though it is more likely an apartment or a house than a traditional office.

With regard to team dynamics, this means that they have moved beyond the stage of a team of sheer equals. The founders are the seniors in the room, and the other early hires are either engineers (the core development team) or generalist assistants for a broad functional area (such as PR, marketing and sales; administration, office manager and receptionist; recruiting and human resources).

DOUG: How do founders manage such a small startup?

ROLAND: In my experience, there is no formal management at all. The team typically has an egalitarian feel to it. You hear founders saying things like "We're all one team here" or "We're a startup, not a bureaucratic corporation." Most will make sure to do their part of the "chores."

DOUG: So no management at all?

ROLAND: There is some management going on, but in a very informal way. Call it a cross between inspiration and apprenticeships.

> *"Management in a startup*
> *is a cross between*
> *inspiration and apprenticeships"*

ROLAND SIEBELINK

Founders typically spend a lot of time getting new team members to buy into the vision, "to drink the Kool Aid" in the words of Silicon Valley. To do so, the team will often socialize together either over the famous two pizzas (Brandt, 2011) or over drinks in a neighborhood bar, where they convince each other time and time again—against all odds—that they are changing the world.

Other than that, founders either "throw employees into the deep" with little guidance, or tell them exactly what to do and how.

DOUG: Do you mean to say that some founders are micromanaging their employees?

Figure 3.2: The Danger of Leading by False Consensus

ROLAND: I do see some micromanagement in this stage, although it is far more common that employees are just "thrown into the deep." This sharp contrast between micromanagement and full delegation is typical of inexperienced managers. Of course, the majority of founders at this stage are twentysomethings, often right out of college, who have never gained management experience.

DOUG: That sounds like managers from hell.

ROLAND: In theory, yes. In practice, at this stage, the management style rarely causes any problems. The trust of working side-by-side with high intensity in a small team makes up for any deficiencies in the way founders are managing their employees.

3.3   Raised Seed Funding

DOUG: How much money have these applicant scaleups raised?

ROLAND: Numbers can differ, both between scaleup companies and across periods of time. It would be typical to have raised between $500K–$1.5M seed money from angels. Perhaps also from some early-stage VCs. This funding has allowed the company to build out their basic team beyond just the founders. At this stage, the bulk of the investment often goes to powering an expanded engineering team.

DOUG: Because building the product is so important at this stage?

ROLAND: Yes indeed, at this stage, it is almost all that matters.

1. Build a prototype into a workable product.

2. Get real users for it and see user traction develop.

3. Turn it into revenue traction.

DOUG: Can startups focus too much on product development?

ROLAND: Yes, that is a great point. Many funded startups overdo the product development phase. One major cause of failure is developing themselves into paralysis (Putorti, 2016).

DOUG: Are they not just trying to impress investors to raise the next round?

ROLAND: They very well may be, but that assumes something. That what got them successful in their Seed funding will also make them successful in their Series A funding. Breaking through that assumpion is one of the hardest lessons to draw from this book. As Marshall Goldsmith and Reiter (2007) famously said:

"What got you here, will not get you there."

MARSHALL GOLDSMITH

DOUG: This does assume that the applicant scaleup has been able to raise some money. Otherwise, how would they pay for all these losses?

ROLAND: Good point! Indeed we have been talking throughout about a tech venture. A growth company that can attract angel money and venture capital. To fund cash flow while it focuses on rapid growth and future product-market-dominance.

DOUG: What is different about other industries then?

ROLAND: Few industries offer the prospect of full product-market-dominance. In most industries, a market leader will always have significant competitors. But in technology (and pharmaceuticals), the winner takes not just the biggest share, but close to 100% of the market. This is why investing in a tech or pharma venture is so attractive to risk-seeking investors. Because the upside is immense.

DOUG: What about startups in other industries, can they attract venture capital?

ROLAND: It is challenging. Elsewhere it is harder to foresee a scalable business model towards future product-market-dominance. In those industries venture capital makes little sense. It is often better to optimize for slower growth, funded by internal cash flow. But those business models are beyond the scope of this book.

DOUG: What if it is a tech company that chooses not to raise any venture funding?

ROLAND: You have to wonder what they are optimizing for. If founders choose not to raise funding, do they not optimize for full control? Rather than maximum scale? It is an early-stage variety of the Rich-versus-Royal dilemma (Wasserman, 2008). Founders can remain absolute monarchs of a small and dying realm. Or they can own a sizable piece of the biggest—and only surviving—realm. Remember that tech industries are winner-takes-all markets. Only the fastest growing rival wins the game.

DOUG: Are there no ventures that were a success despite resisting outside funding?

ROLAND: Of course, there are always exceptions to the rule. Basecamp is one example. A scaleup that enjoyed a great product reputation and nice profitability. But also one where it is hard to argue that they have obtained market leadership in their industry.

Grindr, the LA-based scaleup with a hookup app for gay men, never raised external funding. Until it sold a majority to a Chinese investor in 2017 and the remaining stake in 2018. It is not clear whether raising money for that specific vertical was ever an option. In that case, competitors cannot access venture funds either. This still makes it possible to reach market leadership.

3.4 Reached Problem-Solution-Fit

DOUG: How far are applicant scaleups with their product development?

ROLAND: That can depend very much on the vertical that they are in. Software scaleups tend to have a full working product. Especially if it is a mobile app. Hardware scaleups may still be in a prototype stage. But they are often testing the prototype with real customers in lifelike situations.

DOUG: If the focus is on getting the technology to work, the positioning may not be as mature yet?

ROLAND: You are right. Startups in this stage often have a drive to market an exciting new technology. Engineer-founders, especially, are experts on the technology but not on the use cases.

DOUG: They feel like a solution looking for a problem. What examples would you have of that?

ROLAND: Take the Internet-of-Things ads that AT&T- has been running on season two of the "Masters of Scale" Podcast (Hoffman, 2017b) as a case in point. They start from a vision "Would it not be great if all objects were Internet-enabled." They then struggle to turn that vision into use cases that make an actual difference.

DOUG: Like what, for example?

ROLAND: They are all over the place... One week you hear about IoT helping with digging cables in a city, another week about retracing lost packages, a third week about autonomous cars... All without mentioning alternative solutions already in place to deal with these problems. This is not to talk bad about AT&T—or indeed about *Masters of Scale*, one of my favorite podcasts. I only thought it a typical example of innovator-stage marketing.

DOUG: Thank you for that example. So the answer is to find a specific "problem-solution-fit." What is that, exactly?

ROLAND: We are looking for startups that are solving a problem, not looking for one. A bit of context for that might be useful. The first seed of many startups is fascination with a new technology. Founders then set up a company to work on problems they imagine this technology could solve. In other words, we have a solution looking for a problem.

DOUG: But applicant scaleups have moved on from that initial "find a problem" phase. They have already verified a real-world problem that real customers want solved.

ROLAND: Yes, problem-solution-fit is a defining characteristic of an applicant scaleup. They have narrowed down their options to one verified problem. And they have a working product that is verified to solve it. They are no longer scrambling to discover or serve tens of use cases in parallel.

DOUG: What would be a good example of a startup with problem-solution fit? A team at a stage where they were a clear example of an applicant scaleup?

ROLAND: One company that comes to mind at the time of writing is Netlify. They have built an easy publication workflow for "static websites."

What are static websites *Static websites only serve preprocessed text files, avoiding the overhead of a database. This enables blazing fast web serving. Web developers use Jekyll, Middleman or Hugo to build their site instead of Wordpress. These preprocess dynamic data (such as footers and menus)* *into static text files. The problem is that the output is a bunch of files, and keeping these in sync with your web server is hard.*

Netlify has the best solution for web developers wanting to push a static site onto the web. It integrates with the Github version control technology that developers love. Committing your code pushes your site online. It is a clear problem-solution-fit.

Netlify has signed up 10,000s of users working with those static web technologies. They raised a $12M Series A round from Andreessen Horowitz in 2017. Their next step is to find a subset of customers willing to pay enough for the solution. This is the road to product-market-fit.

3.5 Ensuring the Product is a Pain Killer

DOUG: How easy is it for applicant scaleups to turn problem-solution-fit into product-market-fit?

ROLAND: The difference between problem-solution-fit and product-market-fit is willingness to pay. And for people to be eager to pay, the solution has to take away a real pain in their life. This relates to the famous question, whether your product is a painkiller or a vitamin (Fleming, 2007).

DOUG: What does that mean, a painkiller or a vitamin?

ROLAND: A vitamin is something that may add some extra benefit to your life, but is easy to forego or forget. Something we would put in the "nice to have" category. You hardly notice it when you do not have it.

DOUG: Things like air fresheners, electric toothbrushes, rainproof car mats?

"The difference between problem-solution-fit and
product-market-fit is willingness to pay"

ROLAND SIEBELINK

ROLAND: Yes, you may very well consider those vitamins. But mind you, others may not. No product is always a painkiller or always a vitamin. It depends on the context: on the user, the use case and the alternative. Take a carpal tunnel syndrome patient for example, somebody suffering from painful wrists. Do you think they would consider an electric toothbrush a vitamin or a painkiller?

DOUG: Got it! So painkillers are products that really reduce pain. But for a specific user with a specific problem and a specific alternative.

ROLAND: Yes. Pain in the broadest sense. We talked about avoiding physical pain with an electric toothbrush. But there are many other sorts of pain people want to avoid.

"There are many sorts of pain
that people will pay to avoid"

ROLAND SIEBELINK

1. Feeling ripped off, e.g. by taxis—that pain allowed Uber to disrupt an entire industry;

2. Boredom and annoyance are strong pains in the consumer realm. Witness all the entertainment products that promise to relieve us from it.

3. In business, being responsible for something out of your comfort zone is a huge pain. Hence the many consultants that can serve as a painkiller.

DOUG: That is crystal clear. How many of the applicant scaleups we are talking about have a real painkiller product?

ROLAND: Most will be aware of needing a painkiller. But many of them have not yet reached the sharp value proposition of the absolute pain killer. Getting there will be a major driver in generating revenue traction. And so, in getting closer to raising their Series A.

3.6 Selling to Technology Enthusiasts

DOUG: You mentioned that applicant scaleups have a working product, but not a great positioning yet.

ROLAND: Correct. What matters more than the state of the product is the state of the adoption curve. And the kind of customers these scale-ups have to target at each stage. Moore (2013) has long taught that the techology adoption cycle is key to successful tech marketing.

DOUG: OK then! What kind of customer should I expect to find at an applicant scaleup?

ROLAND: At this early stage, we find a majority of "techie" customers. People that like and appreciate the technology for its own sake and would

Four Decisions™ Tech Edition Tools: Strategy Decision

State of the ScaleUp—Extrapolating Current Reality into the Future

Scale-up Ally

Keep growing, keep your culture

Instructions:

1. The objective of this exercise is to get a *nuanced but realistic assessment* on what the future of the company will look like if nothing changes from what we are doing now.
2. To make sure the assessment is balanced, we want everyone to *apply different perspectives* using the "six thinking hats" (Edward de Bono), see below.
3. Answer individually: wearing this hat, based on this perspective, what will our business look like in three years if we just keep doing what we are doing now (no change)? • focus on extrapolating *current* business activities/behaviors/strengths/weaknesses, *not future plans* • however, you may include projects/programs/initiatives that are *almost finished.*
4. Discuss as a group, bringing together your insights one-hat-at-a-time.

White hat: based on the facts, just the facts available, what will the business look like in 3 years with no change?	**Red hat:** based on your intuition, feelings, loves, hates, what will the business look like in 3 years with no change?
Black hat: looking at caveats, risks and negatives, what will the business look like in 3 years with no change?	**Green hat:** based on creative possibilities, alternatives, what will the business look like in 3 years with no change?
Yellow hat: looking at positives, value and benefits, what will the business look like in 3 years with no change?	**Blue hat: based on insights generated here,** what can we learn from this process? How should we proceed?

Figure 3.3: Worksheet: Aligning your Team on the Current Reality

like to experiment with it. In line with the technology adoption curve, we call these users "Innovators."

Innovators get excited about the broad potential of a technology. Not so much about any particular business case. They may be opinion leaders in their technology field. But from a business point-of-view they are more inventors than serious business users.

DOUG: Can you give me an example of technologies that are still in the *innovator stage?*

ROLAND: Yes, if you will allow that things may have changed since we wrote this book. But at the time of writing, typical technologies in the *innovator-stage* are:

1. the Internet of Things;

2. Augmented Reality;

3. the Blockchain–as a generic technology beyond cryptocurrencies.

DOUG: How do you recognize which technologies are still in the innovator stage?

ROLAND: I find there are several good indicators of these technologies:

1. They excite many engineers;

2. Technical publications cover them extensively;

3. Their marketing that sounds limitless. "Look at the endless possibilities that this technology brings!"

For example, when I worked at Topicmarks, we had an amazing summarization algorithm. It could summarize a PDF of a thousand pages in seconds. But we listed many use cases in different verticals. Students, lawyers, researchers, managers. Many possibilities but no focus on a single use case.

"Innovators serve a key function in vetting a technology for Early Adopters"

AFTER GEOFFREY MOORE

DOUG: How do applicant scaleups market their product to these Innovators?

ROLAND: Innovators serve a key function in vetting the technology for Early Adopters. These form the next stage of the technology adoption curve, and the first market with money. But Early Adopters will only buy if Innovators have vetted the technology as working.

DOUG: Is that why so much of tech startup's marketing collateral is technology-driven?

ROLAND: Indeed. It is trying to excite technologists about the potential of a technology per se. And showing that it got that technology to work. So that Innovators will no longer serve as a gatekeeper. They can recommend the technology to business users that could use the product.

DOUG: Why would a technologist serve as a gatekeeper? Who prevents business users or consumers from installing the app they want to try?

ROLAND: The role of the innovator as a "hard" gatekeeper has diminished. In line with the rise of the cloud, smartphone apps and "bring your own device" policies. In B2B, these trends have weakened many controls that IT departments had in place. As such, SAAS and smartphone revolutions have solved a major go-to-market bottleneck.

Yet targeting Innovators is still important to overcome "soft gate-keeping." Innovators will still influence what other people try out or not. They are often the opinion leaders that make Early Adopters aware that a new product even exists.

3.7 Establishing Revenue Traction

DOUG: What competences does an applicant scaleup need? To move to the next stage and become a proper scaleup?

ROLAND: There is only one competence that stands out for applicant scaleups. To turn traction into revenues. Revenue indicates that the company has found at least some degree of product-market-fit. This makes it ready to leave the startup stage and move to the scaleup stage.

DOUG: Let us first talk about traction for a second. How do you define traction and what kinds of traction are there?

ROLAND: Traction means that the market is responding to your efforts in increasing numbers. It can apply to users, to revenue, and other forms of market feedback. In Silicon Valley, the term also implies that the market response is bigger than the efforts you put in.

DOUG: When do you recognize user traction?

ROLAND: When the growth of the user base is higher than the percentage of users that are churning. In other words, the total user base keeps growing.

DOUG: What about revenue traction?

ROLAND: When the total deal volume keeps increasing, after subtracting non-renewed revenue.

DOUG: What about other forms of traction?

ROLAND: You can expand the concept of traction across other categories. For example: investor traction, strategic partner traction, job applicant traction. Good applicant scaleups need some traction in all these.

"User traction is paramount because
it proves the desirability of the product."

ROLAND SIEBELINK

DOUG: Why is user traction so important?

ROLAND: Because it is the ultimate proof of the desirability of the product. It does not matter if we think that AirBnB is a crazy idea. As many of the first venture capitalists exposed to the idea did. The fact is that it is attracting an ever growing base of users.

Traction also indicates some form of autonomous growth. This implies extrapolation to huge numbers in the future. It means that the product is very compelling. So compelling, that people keep using it and tell their friends.

For revenue traction, it means that new customers and deals are coming in "without effort." Or at the least, without it feeling like an "uphill battle" for your sales channels.

DOUG: Then traction must be a paramount metric for investors.

ROLAND: It is, especially at the early stage. Traction is the only thing that closes deals with early-stage-investors. Though they will of course also look at the team and the product.

> *"Only traction closes a round*
> *with early-stage investors"*
>
> ROLAND SIEBELINK

DOUG: How does a startup go about creating traction and revenues?

ROLAND: That question is so well covered in the startup literature out there. Ries (2011) aggregated all the best early-stage startup advice from Silicon Valley. Then turned it into *Lean Startup*, "the startup Bible." The book is all about turning your ideas for a startup into real traction.

DOUG: For those that do not have the book at hand, what is a quick summary?

ROLAND: Iterating through the following steps:

1. Plan your hypotheses.

2. Get out of the building to test them,

3. and then to learn from your results,

4. to generate a next round of hypotheses.

DOUG: So the end result is just a new round of hypotheses?

ROLAND: Hypotheses are intermediate results. End results are always measured as traction. First, you need to show user traction. Then several next rounds of experiments will bring about some revenues. Successful monetization, even at small scale, proves product-market-fit.

DOUG: What about competences in team management, strategy, execution or financial prudence?

ROLAND: This may sound controversial. But at this early stage, none of these really matter. Unless the company has first mastered reaching product-market-fit.

"In the early stage, traditional management skills hardly matter."

ROLAND SIEBELINK

DOUG: What about raising money, building a team, designing your business model? Are these not crucial to building reaching scaleup status?

ROLAND: For certain, founders will find much guidance out there. How to connect with angels, how to pitch to VCs, how to draw up your business model canvas... (Osterwalder and Pigneur, 2009). But in my experience, startups ready for the scaleup phase have one thing in common. They have all reached product-market-fit.

They do not have in common that they are the best networkers, that they are great at pitching to VCs. Let alone that they have a brilliant business model canvas. All these things may help. To get more insights into the target markets. To bring the company closer to traction and revenues. But in the end they are side stories.

DOUG: So product-market-fit is really all that matters.

ROLAND: Correct, and the proof of product-market-fit is revenue traction. When considering to work with an applicant scaleup, I always look for traction. With more users coming back than churning. And with more paying customers signing up than are canceling. This is an indicator they can to turn the value they have created into some profitable growth.

3.8 Getting Ready to Raise Series A

DOUG: Once an applicant scaleup has mastered these competences, are they ready for Series A?

ROLAND: They are much more likely to get interest for their series A. On top of that, they are much more likely to turn the raise into a success. The main purpose of Series A, as you will remember, is to build a solid "go-to-market." This is Silicon-Valley-speak for a successful marketing-and-sales-machine.

DOUG: You mentioned some underlying success drivers like functional alignment, core identity and cross-functional priorities. How do they help with that goal?

ROLAND: They are the powers to build a solid go-to-market with.

1. Embracing the core identity (Collins, 2001), helps to design a clear go-to-market strategy. The team will find it easier to agree

on a single core customer and distinctive brand promises. This
will reassure investors that the company will reach a defensible
position fast. It will not waste precious resources on trying to boil
the marketing ocean.

2. Strong functional alignment makes it easier to design an attractive value proposition together. One you find enough customers
for. One where everything works at levels the customer is expecting. One where you get paid more than what it costs to produce
the product. This will make the future economics look great in
investors' eyes.

3. Mastering cross-functional priorities means resolving day-to-day
tactical dependence on the Founder/CEO. Other team members
are now empowered to lead and deliver initiatives. The company
can deliver several things in parallel. This means an immediate
boost in execution effectiveness. The Founder/CEO can start de-
pending on the organization delivering their priorities. This can
free up to 80% of their time for market-facing activities. Such
as strategic partnerships, important customer deals and raising
money.

DOUG: What key points should the Series A pitch contain?

ROLAND: In a series A pitch, investors look most for solid revenue traction. Especially that there is a large share of returning users, who also
refer their friends. Strong painkiller scores (see previous chapter) tend to
drive this stickiness. Strong net promoter scores (over 50) drive revenue
growth through referrals. Two supporting "promises" in a series A pitch
would be percent gross profit and market size.

1. Percent gross profit shows that the customers' willingness to pay is high enough to cover the base production costs.

2. Market size shows that the revenue potential is far bigger than the current (test) customer base.

4

Freshman Scaleups: Mastering Distribution

DOUG: Freshman Scaleups! Now we are moving into true scaleup territory!

ROLAND: Yes, this is where we enter the real program. Our former startups and applicant scaleups have now become freshman scaleups.

DOUG: And about time too! In this chapter, I want to get to the bottom of freshman scaleups. I have so many questions about:

- the people in a freshman scaleup;

- their starting situation and challenge;

- what their key goal for this stage should be;

- how they should best go about reaching that goal;

- in which market(s) they should concentrate;

- what business value this could add;

- and what a typical timeline is to raise the next series.

ROLAND: Of course! We will cover all these questions and many more. But the main thing I want to cover is the key challenge for scaleups at this stage: mastering distribution.

DOUG: What do you mean with that? Setting up all kinds of sales channels?

ROLAND: Not quite yet. One channel is usually enough at this stage. As long as the company figures out how to make the cost to acquire a customer lower than the expected lifetime value of that customer. We will come back to that later in this chapter.

4.1 Beyond Product-Market-Fit

DOUG: Your definition of a scaleup requires that it is beyond product-market-fit. How exactly do you define that milestone?

ROLAND: For a company to be beyond product-market-fit, it must meet two conditions.

1. Significant product dependence.

2. Customers showing willingness to pay above cost.

DOUG: What do you mean with product dependence?

ROLAND: That the product must be a superior solution to an existing problem. So superior, that at least 40% of users become dependent on

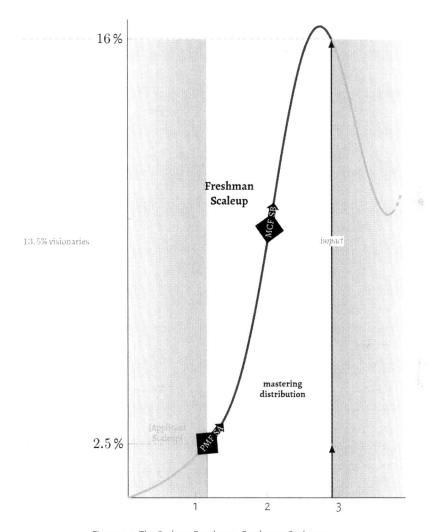

16 %

13.5% visionaries

Freshman Scaleup

MCF SF

impact

mastering
distribution

[Applicant Scaleup]

PMF SA

2.5 %

1   2   3

Figure 4.1: The Scaleup Roadmap: Freshman Scaleups

the product. This means they "would be very disappointed if the product were no longer available" (Marmer et al., 2011).

DOUG: This is what we called problem–solution-fit, right?

ROLAND: Correct. With the caveat that we are now talking about a real, working product. We are not in prototype territory anymore.

But product-market-fit goes one level deeper. The company also has to generate revenue from this problem-solution-fit. In other words, at least some customers are happy to pay for the solution.

> *"Product-market-fit implies*
> *customers willling to pay."*
>
> ROLAND SIEBELINK

DOUG: On the "willingness to pay" criterion, how much should customers pay, before you can acknowledge product-market-fit?

ROLAND: The baseline is that the revenue covers marginal production cost. In other words, if one additional unit of product for one additional customer costs $1 to produce, the scaleup should charge the customer more than $1.

If a startup got traction by selling below marginal cost, I would not declare product-market-fit yet. But it is fine not to cover other costs like sales, general and administrative cost yet. That comes later.

DOUG: Still, many startups made their start in selling products at low prices. Even giving them away for free. Reid Hoffman says that, in winner-takes-all markets, that is actually the smart thing to do (Hoffman, 2018).

ROLAND: Absolutely. Price competition can be an effective entry strategy into saturated markets. If tech scaleups strived to be profitable from day one, they would never make enough of a dent. To disrupt their industry, they will need to establish a radical value proposition. Often that includes radical price reductions, especially early in the innovation curve.

DOUG: So it is okay for startups to offer products for free or compete with heavy discounts?

ROLAND: Every startup can of course do what it likes. But often, scaleups with free offerings have a different customer in mind than the user.

A case in point is Google. In their early days, they tried to charge enterprise customers to use their search engine. Then they moved towards a free model that would be available to all consumers. Making their search engine free of course helped to establish tremendous traction. But more importantly, it helped them establish a new business model. Letting advertisers reach consumers at the moment they express interest in a product.

DOUG: Which has become a very profitable business model for Google...

ROLAND: Very profitable indeed! This story illustrates why scaleups rarely care about profitability in the short term. What matters is establishing a new business model. It may take significant investment up front. But it should generate outsized revenue growth and profits over time.

DOUG: So would you say that Google reached product-market-fit without any revenues?

ROLAND: Not without any revenues, no. Product-market-fit only occurred once the first advertisers started paying for click-throughs.

> *"If you are not paying for it,*
> *you are not the customer.*
> *You are the product being sold."*
>
> ANDREW LEWIS

4.2   Raising Series A

DOUG: How about raising money in the freshman scaleup stage?

ROLAND: It becomes a lot easier. As a startup, the business already had problem-solution-fit, with clear user traction established. That allowed it to raise angel money. Now it is starting to show product-market-fit, with clear revenue traction. This represents a major de-risking of the business proposition. Enough for venture capital funds to flow in, with bigger checks.

DOUG: That must be a big relief to the founders.

ROLAND: It can be, if:

1. the revenue traction is obvious,

2. the seed round's angel investors are well-regarded in Silcon Valley, and

3. they all want to follow-up in Series A.

DOUG: Raising Series A is not as easy as the stories make it sound, though.

ROLAND: You hear many fundraising stories while networking and read them in *TechCrunch*. All show survivor bias and lots of retroactive PR-editing. Our chart in the first chapter showed that only 46% of seed-funded companies raise a Series A round (CB Insights, 2017).

> *"Only 46% of seed-funded companies*
> *raise a Series A round"*
>
> CB INSIGHTS

If your scaleup is among the lucky 40%, though, you will experience $2–10 million coming in. That means hiring more people, a better office, proper salaries for the founders. In other words: a feeling like "you've made it."

DOUG: I'm sure the Porsche and Ferrari dealers cannot wait for companies to raise their Series A.

ROLAND: Not so fast... At this stage, experienced VCs are quite careful with actually disbursing the funds. They will set up several internal milestones that the company needs to reach. New tranches of cash to the company are conditional on these milestones. Only when a venture raises Series B can founders sell some of their stock for cash. And buy the car of their dreams.

4.3 Structuring a Family-Sized Team

DOUG: Can we look at the size of the company first? You called freshman scaleups family-sized. I guess you mean an extended family?

ROLAND: Yes, this is a slight variation on the terminology the *Blitzscaling* course at Stanford used (Townsend, 2015). Family-sized is one level higher than household-sized. It refers to an extended family of up to 30 people living/working under the same roof.

DOUG: There is a big difference between a team of 10 and a team of 30, though.

ROLAND: Indeed there is. You can still manage a team of 10 like the household-sized team we discovered in the previous chapter. But as it grows to add more hires, it starts to have a need for management structure and the first signs of hierarchy.

- With a team of 10 people, it feels natural to take all decisions together. Everybody discusses around the table, regardless of rank.

- With a team of 20, that feels awkward. Many people dare not speak up or feel like they are wasting their time in the meeting.

- With a team of 30, it becomes downright unproductive to maintain a full democracy. The bigger team needs more separation of concerns.

DOUG: How do you see freshman scaleups structuring themselves in this phase?

*"With a team of 30, democracy
becomes downright unproductive."*

ROLAND SIEBELINK

ROLAND: The key is for the founders to hire senior enough people to delegate an entire functional area to. See the A-player hiring tools on pages 118–119. Good founders grow aware where their own functional expertise may fall short. They should be eager to hire experts for the areas that they feel uncomfortable managing.

DOUG: What does this mean in practice?

ROLAND: Each cofounder hires a senior enough person to manage each of the functions that they themselves are still responsible for. For example, a business founder/CEO will hire a sales manager, customer success manager and a marketing manager. Perhaps also a finance/HR manager before they can afford a CFO. The CTO will hire an engineering manager, an operations manager, a product manager etc.

DOUG: Are these all VP level people?

ROLAND: Not necessarily. Some of them will have VP titles, some of them Director titles. Key is that they are able to manage an area on their own. And that they are able to coach a flat team of junior people directly. The goal is that the founder(s) need no longer be involved in functional decision-making.

DOUG: So what are your recommendations?

ROLAND: They are simple. In this stage I recommend:

Preparing to Hire an A-Player: Scorecard and Sourcing

Role: _____

Reports to: _____

Hiring A-Players: Right People on the Bus

Scale-ups that want to outperform their competition have an intentional process to hire 90% A-players:

- Can do the job while fitting in with the culture.
- Has _at least 90% chance_ of achieving a set of outcomes
- that _only the top 10% of candidates_ could achieve
- within the salary/budget available for the position.

A disciplined hiring process avoids _voodoo hiring._

1. Instructions: Scorecard

- Individually, define the mission of the role. Keep it precise, plain and short:

- As a group, discuss and finalize:

2. Instructions: Sourcing

- Individually, brainstorm about all the ways to source from your networks:

- As a group, identify top 3 actions to source from your networks:

- One person to fill out _Who Scorecard_ tool from http://geoffsmart.com/smarttools/ ◉

Who draws up full scorecard: _____

People to sign off on full scorecard: _____

Figure 4.2: Worksheet: A-Players—Scorecard and Sourcing

Preparing to Hire an A-Player: Disciplined Selection Process

Scale-up Ally △
helping tech founders scale with success

Role:

Reports to:

☐ Scorecard tool discussed and attached
☐ Compensation range discussed and attached

1. Screening interviews (quick)
☐ Hiring manager
☐ Using *only* the *Who* Screening tool ⊙

Date	Candidate	A–C

2. Tandem *Who* interviews (4h)
☐ Hiring manager and _
☐ Using *only* the *Who* Interview tool ⊙

Date	Candidate/Notes	A–C

3. Focused interviews (1h each)
☐ Involving other interviewers
☐ Using *only* the *Who* Focused interview tool ⊙

Inter-viewer	Predefined topic	Notes	A–C

4. Reference Calls: fail former bosses
☐ Split between tandem interviewers
☐ Using *only* the *Who* Reference tool ⊙

5. Decide whom to hire
☐ Manager extends offer with permission from CEO/Head HR
☐ Using the *Who* Sell Tool ⊙

Adapted from *Who - The A Method for Hiring* by Geoff Smart and Randy Street

©Scale-Up Allies LLC. All Rights Reserved.

Figure 4.3: Worksheet: A-Players—Selection and Selling

"The goal is that founder(s) need to be involved
only in cross-functional decisions"

ROLAND SIEBELINK

1. Keeping the organization flat: no more than two levels below the founder/C-suite level.

2. Assuming there is more than one founder: sharing the burden of direct reports between the founders.

3. Engineering and sales are the two heavyweight teams in a freshman scaleup. They should report to different founders.

4.4   Capturing Market Imagination

DOUG: Let us move to the results side. The key challenge in this stage is mastering distribution. So what of growth rates and sales should we expect to see in a freshman scaleup?

ROLAND: Freshman tech scaleups are starting to capture the market imagination, so we look for sales multiplying. Doubling, tripling or even quadrupling sales in this first year is normal. Especially when many freshman scaleups start from such a low base.

DOUG: Verne Harnish considers any company that grows more than 20% a year a scaleup (Harnish, 2014). 20% is much lower than what you mention.

"Tech scaleups need to grow by factors faster than scaleups in other industries"

ROLAND SIEBELINK

ROLAND: It is. Verne's definition reflects that he works across industries. 20% is challenging in traditional industries such as hospitality, construction and consulting. But it is too little when you can leverage the extreme scalability of tech businesses. In tech, the stakes and the payoff are much higher because of the winner-takes-all nature.

DOUG: But how is it even possible to sustain such high sales growth? Who could multiply their sales team several times over in a year? And still keep up the quality and its culture?

ROLAND: Remember, we are still in the freshman scaleup stage. We are talking about companies with revenues around $1 million. Most have large online components to the sales process. They also have a high degree of user referrals. The scaleup has built significant user traction in the problem-solution-fit stage. At least 40% of its users state that they "would be very disappointed if the product were no longer available" (Marmer et al., 2011).

DOUG: They may not actually have a proper sales force yet.

ROLAND: That is so true. The founders are often doing most of the sales. Many sales come from overenthusiastic early adopter users. The founders are lucky if they can afford one marketing/sales/growth/business development assistant.

DOUG: You also mentioned "plenty of promoters." I would imagine the start up/scaleup has had to be great at self-promotion for quite a while now to make it this far?

ROLAND: Absolutely. No growth company can make it to this stage without a healthy appetite for self-promotion. Rei Inamoto (Vangool, 2011) and Dave McClure (Tsotsis, 2011) call the startup CEO "the hustler." This is exactly what they mean. People who get into an accelerator without fulfilling the requirements. Who somehow talk themselves into a room with important investors. Who find a way to get an article into *TechCrunch*.

DOUG: I have seen that "hustle" at a much earlier stage.

ROLAND: You are right, it has to be there from the beginning. The difference here is that external people are starting to promote the scaleup. A freshman scaleup gets the attention from people scouting for the next big thing. Influencers are starting to carry the banner of the company, often unpaid.

DOUG: Why would people who are not paid by the scaleup want to promote it?

ROLAND: Because by now, the company has reached the stage of "the next cool thing." The people are promoting the scaleup not out of interest for the company per se. But because they always identify the next cool thing and have a reputation to uphold. For their readers, for their viewers, for their executives, for their funds.

DOUG: I understand promoters are a nice thing to have, but are we not devoting a bit too much space to them? Who needs promoters when you have advertising?

ROLAND: It is true that there are many more marketing options out there than even ten years ago. People now set up their own campaigns online with ease. And with digital marketing, everything has become measurable. All these things can make us forget that marketing remains an expensive activity. Getting enough results out of a paid campaign often feels like an uphill battle.

DOUG: Good campaign analysts providing recommendations based on the learning are invaluable to make paid advertising work.

"You need promoters for your
paid marketing campaigns to become efficient"

DOUG MILLER

ROLAND: They are. On top of that, founders fail to realize that good marketing strategies only become great with referrals. Marketing can do little by itself if customers do not trust the product yet. Trust comes when current customers recommend the product to their friends and acquaintances. Or sometimes when influencers create product awareness among the fans that trust them.

DOUG: So you need promoters for your paid marketing campaigns to become efficient.

ROLAND: That is my take on it. With referrals and endorsements in place, marketing benefits from a snowball effect. It is this kind of efficient marketing a scaleup will need to master before they can raise their series B.

4.5 Selling to Visionary Business Users

DOUG: Freshman scaleups are no longer targeting innovators. What changes when they sell to early-adopter customers?

ROLAND: Unlike Innovators, Early Adopter-type customers are not excited about technology per se. Their focus is on the opportunity to gain an advantage over their competition. And how the new technology or product can give them a leg up with that. Moore (2013) often refers to these customers as "visionaries." They buy into the vision of the product before the product delivers on it in full. Or sometimes they have stronger visions for the product than the founders themselves.

DOUG: Sounds like they are the perfect match for your archetypal tech entrepreneur.

> *"Visionary users are the customers*
> *tech entrepreneurs most relate to"*

ROLAND SIEBELINK

ROLAND: They are, at least for the founder that is business-focused (often the CEO or the "hustler"). This is the kind of customer that founders most relate to. The person who shares their product vision long before the full benefit is there. Who is willing to support them now, even if the product has realized only part of that vision.

But this is not the ideal customer for the more technology-focused founders (often the CTO). CTOs are usually more comfortable speaking to Innovator-type customers. People excited about the technology per se.

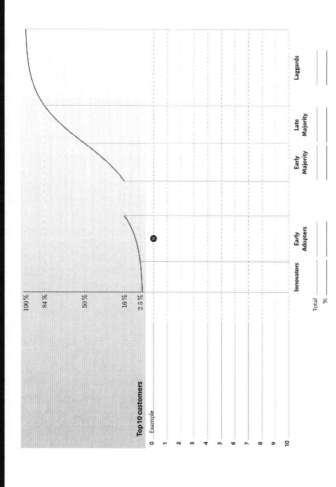

Top 10 customers	Innovators	Early Adopters	Early Majority	Late Majority	Laggards
0 Example					
1					
2					
3					
4					
5					
6					
7					
8					
9					
10					
Total					
%					

Source: Roland Siebelink, after Geoffrey Moore.

Figure 4.4: Worksheet: Technology Adoption Curve

DOUG: So you get CEOs talking to visionaries and CTOs to technology enthusiasts.

ROLAND: That is the risk. You can imagine how this can derail customer development. When different founders get feedback from different phase customers.

DOUG: So it is important for the entire team to align on what phase they are in.

ROLAND: And what phase is their next challenge! What type of customer is going to have to be their main source of growth in the next year? If it is innovators then everybody should talk only to innovators. If it is early adopters then everybody should talk only to early adopters.

Without agreement on the customer targeted, innovation and acquisition will not match up. The product pipeline will clog up with esoteric feature requests from Innovators. While sales will fall short of target because Early Adopters cannot get a project in.

DOUG: Our *Technology Adoption Curve* worksheet on page 125 helps coaches align their scaleup teams on where they are positioned.

ROLAND: Correct. It lets the team map current customers to the five adoption phases of Moore (2013)'s technology adoption curve. And then determine where the majority of customers is at. I recommend coaches of tech scaleups spend 60–90 minutes on it in each annual planning session.

4.6 Repeatable, Profitable Sales

DOUG: The essence of mastering distribution is to generate repeatable, profitable sales, is that right?

ROLAND: That is the idea. Repeatable, profitable sales are the key milestone that freshman scaleups need to reach. On their way to becoming a sophomore scaleup. And to product-market dominance.

DOUG: We have talked about sales profitability, but what about repeatability?

ROLAND: It will not surprise you that repeatability is absolute key in the scaleup stage. And what is more, repeatability without assuming that your tenth hire will be as effective as your first hire. As Jon Kondo of OpsPanda has discovered, this is where many sales plans stumble (Siebelink, 2017b).

DOUG: Does that not smack too much of routine for the average startup team?

ROLAND: That is a great question! It illustrates why I prefer to call these companies scaleups, not startups anymore. In an early-stage startup, people abhor repeatability and routine. Its whole idea is to *disrupt* something repeatable and routine. Something that we have all gotten used to.

DOUG: But what happens once the startup has found that disruptive offering and the market buys it?

ROLAND: The rational course of action is to build momentum around the offering it has brought to market. Not to keep reinventing and disrupting other markets. Not before the initial disruption has realized its potential.

"Routine and Repeatability:
The Death of Startups—
But the Lifeblood of Scaleups"

ROLAND SIEBELINK

In other words, repeatability and routine are death for startups. But they are the lifeblood of scaleups. And of course, some team members may have trouble adapting to that new reality.

DOUG: What is the financial state of a freshman scaleup? I mean, what financial criteria should they meet to be a "proper" freshman scaleup?

ROLAND: As we said under product-market-fit, the key is to have revenues. Not any revenues—consulting gigs etc. do not count. We need to see revenues from sales of the product the team has developed. In other words, the freshman scaleup has initial customers with willingness to pay.

DOUG: How much revenue? What if the revenues are very low? Sometimes they seem negligible compared to the burn rate the freshman scaleup incurs...

ROLAND: That is OK for now. In the freshman stage, we do not particularly care about any profitability metrics.

DOUG: The only red flag is when the freshman scaleup is selling its products below cost.

ROLAND: Yes, when the price it charges for the product is much lower than the cost it incurs to produce one. We do like to see at least a gross profit on the product that the scaleup sells.

But any profit focus beyond that, and we get worried. Because premature profit optimization can strangle the optimization for rapid growth.

"Premature profit optimization can strangle the optimization for rapid growth"

ROLAND SIEBELINK

DOUG: This focus on profitable sales did surprise me a bit. You mentioned that you do not particularly care about profitability in tech scaleups. And yet you mentioned "gross profit" as a requirement even for freshman scaleups. What gives?

ROLAND: Good catch. For tech companies with venture funding, we rarely look at short-term profitability. This is because the payoff of becoming market leader is so much greater. In a tech scaleup, any focus away from capturing the market opportunity is sure to destroy value.

But a scaleup also has to show increasing financial competence over a startup. Some freshman scaleups sell a product unit for less than it costs to produce that unit. While this can be a market entry strategy, venture investors will want it fixed as soon as possible. The next round investment depends on the freshman scaleup reaching unit profitability.

DOUG: Why can they not delay unit profitability until they are a sophomore scaleup?

Your Power of One		Net Cash Flow $	EBIT $
Your Current Position			

Your Power of One	Change you would like to make	Annual Impact on Cash Flow $	Impact on EBIT $
Price Increase %	1 %		
Volume Increase %	1 %		
COGS Reduction %	1 %		
Overheads Reduction %	1 %		
Reduction in Debtors Days	1 days		
Reduction in Stock Days	1 days		
Increase in Creditors Days	1 days		
Your Power of One Impact		0	0

Your Power of One		Net Cash Flow $	EBIT $
Your Adjusted Position		0	0

Figure 4.5: Gazelles Worksheet: "Power of One"

ROLAND: Because a sophomore scaleup focuses on building up efficient distribution. It has no time to also optimize production processes. The risk is that it scales its sales and marketing on the back of a loss-making product. In other words, it scales massive losses.

That is why reaching unit profitability is a basic financial competence. One we should expect of a freshman scaleup team. The minimal need is to capture more revenue per unit of product than the cost required to produce it.

"Without gross margin, the company risks scaling massive losses"

ROLAND SIEBELINK

DOUG: So it is more about projections and less about cash flow?

ROLAND: That is exactly right. Let engineering and operations work towards a scalable production model. Let sales and marketing work towards a scalable sales model. In the same way, let finance and management work towards a scalable business model. One that produces sizable profit when the market opportunity has been captured and the business has reached scale.

That does not mean the scaleup has to be profitable today, far from it. But it does mean that management has to gain the ability to project future finances. Of large market opportunities and sustainable, profitable growth far out into the future.

4.7 Optimizing for Rapid Growth

DOUG: Moving away from the finances, what is the mood in the typical freshman scaleup? How are they mastering distribution?

ROLAND: By definition, a new scaleup has recently found product-market-fit. This has caused fast increase in demand, in investor money, and in resources needed. The business is scrambling to keep up with customer demand, and hiring new resources as fast as it can. Often, maintaining that growth and hiring for it become ends unto themselves.

DOUG: I should hope so! The faster it grows, the faster it can dominate the market.

ROLAND: You would think so. If only its founders were aware of that goal of establishing dominance. The tragedy is that many are not.

> *"The biggest scaleup risk is*
> *growth from any source at any cost"*

ROLAND SIEBELINK

DOUG: Really? Then what do scaleups focus on after they have reached product-market-fit?

ROLAND: Most common is a focus on growth per se, from any source and at any cost. As long as top line revenues keep growing, it is easy to keep finding new venture capital. But unless the company disciplines the kind of business it is in, it grows in size without growing in power.

DOUG: Can you explain that more, growing in size without growing in power?

ROLAND: I often use the analogy of a weight lifter and a body builder. Size matters in that they both have bulky bodies. But the weight lifter knows his goal is to build strength (market power). The bodybuilder focuses on size (growth) per se, and would lose in a direct contest.

DOUG: So it is not size that matters, it is market power and speed. Why?

ROLAND: Because any scaleup is in a race with incumbents. The scaleup needs to grab market share before the incumbents can copy the innovation. It is like a gazelle that has to keep running all day to stay ahead of the predators.

'The battle between every startup and
incumbent comes down to
whether the startup gets the distribution
before the incumbent gets the innovation."

ALEX RAMPELL

DOUG: So healthy growth means reinforcing that market power and speed.

ROLAND: For example by entrenching itself deeper and deeper into its core product-market-segment. Unhealthy growth keeps weakening the market power and speed. For example, by expanding into too many adjacent businesses at once. Losing discipline about understanding true customer needs. And complicating decision-making long before the scaleup has gotten anywhere near the weight of incumbency.

4.8 Clarifying the Core Decisions

DOUG: This brings us to the rising confusion and friction that often accompany scaleups. What if people cannot agree about who is accountable for what?

ROLAND: I have encountered this with a few clients. Almost always, there are underlying trust issues. People fear the direction peers wanted to take the company in. So they resist delegation of accountability to these peers.

DOUG: So fear is driving disempowerment! Interesting, I have never looked at it that way. How else does this manifest itself?

ROLAND: Founders often experience it as "threading water." They hire many more people to cover more ground faster.

DOUG: And all they get is everyone slowing down. Why?

ROLAND: There are several issues at work here.

Confusion about top priorities People feel confused about their top priorities. With all the new people added, does everyone still know what to focus their day on and where to make most headway?

Premature complexity Founders' creativity and penchant for new products may have added premature complexity. Is every department spreading their time across all products? And are these products serving the same customer or different ones? How do people choose which customer request is most important to attend to?

Degree of responsiveness How responsive is the scaleup to the market? When customer requests come in, how many decisions can people take at the front line? How many need to go to managers or even executives to arbitrate? How much is that slowing people down?

DOUG: Somehow, adding more people does not result in being able to do more things...

ROLAND: I could not have put it better. If you think about it, "doing more things" means scaling the capacity of the organization to do things. And that means scaling the capacity to take decisions. Not big strategic decisions but small tactical decisions:

- whether to work on product feature A or B;

- what to charge customer C;

- how much to compensate customer D with for an error made;

- how to adapt the value proposition for a new segment;

- whether to accept payments through a new channel.

The more decision capacity, the more market segments the company can be successful in. The more customers it can sign up and serve over the competition. To increase that capacity, we not only need more people. We also need the mechanisms that allow them to take decisions.

DOUG: What mechanisms are you thinking about?

ROLAND: We already discussed functional accountability. But even more importantly. Confirm your core values and purpose. Define your core customer. Set clear functional and product accountability. Draw up joint priorities for the organization at large.

DOUG: Interesting! How do you solve such a problem?

ROLAND: In these situations, the team needs to ensure it agrees on the "broad lines" first. I recommend starting all the way back with the most fundamental question: do we agree on our core values? Our core purpose? Are the beliefs we share about how people should behave and what we are trying to create aligned? See our Strategy Vision Summary worksheet on page 137. Based on the Gazelles worksheet with the same name, can help you answer and communicate these core decisions.

DOUG: Once you have those broad lines in place, it becomes easier to align on longer term priorities.

ROLAND: And then, to break these down into annual and quarterly priorities. Even to pick one key performance metric (critical number). Not departmental purpose, priorities and metrics, mind you! But purpose, priorities and metrics for the organization at large.

DOUG: Why not have departmental priorities and metrics?

ROLAND: Every department can have priorities and metrics, of course, and should. My point is not to treat the company priorities and metrics as the mere sum of the departmental ones. Instead, it should be the other way around. The company should set overarching cross-functional priorities and metrics first. And then departments should set their own priorities and metrics. To drive what the company is trying to achieve (Siebelink, 2009).

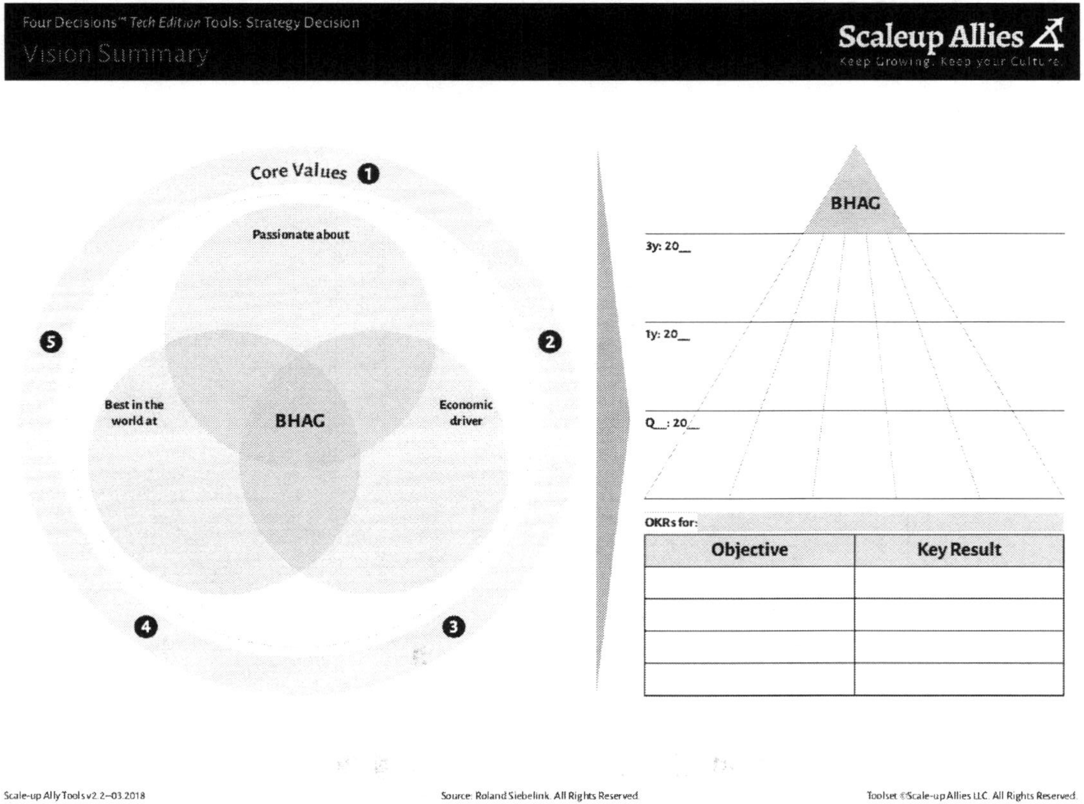
Four Decisions™ Tech Edition Tools: Strategy Decision
Vision Summary
Scaleup Allies
Keep Growing. Keep your Culture.
Core Values 1
Passionate about
Best in the world at
BHAG
Economic driver
2
3
4
5
BHAG
3y: 20__
1y: 20__
Q__: 20__
OKRs for:
Objective
Key Result
Scale-up Ally Tools v2.2–03.2018
Source: Roland Siebelink. All Rights Reserved.
Toolset ©Scale-up Allies LLC. All Rights Reserved.

Figure 4.6: Worksheet: Strategy Vision Summary

DOUG: If done well, this must liberate an enormous amount of energy.

ROLAND: I have seen this happen many times. You will enjoy an immediate leap in productivity and motivation. The more you focus on core decisions and overarching priorities, the more you will get back to the startup pace you once had.

4.9   Mastering Distribution: CLV > CAC

DOUG: The company has reached solid product-market-fit to reach the freshman scaleup stage. But to truly master distribution, they need to reach market-channel-fit?

ROLAND: Yes. Now it is no longer about nurturing customers willing to pay for the product. It is about reaching those customers through your sales channels in an efficient way. "Efficient," in this context, means at a profit. The cost to make the sale should be lower than the lifetime value the customer will generate for you.

DOUG: I have heard that are many different definitions of customer lifetime value (CLV).

ROLAND: The exact CLV calculation depends on the value proposition of the company. And early in its history, there must be a large speculative component about the future. But generally, one can calculate CLV as:

1. cumulative operating profits from the average customer,

2. over the time that you expect that average customer to stay with you.

DOUG: How does the choice of channel impact this?

ROLAND: You can think of a continuum of marketing and sales channels:

- with low cost/high-volume transactional sales channels at the beginning of the axis.

- and high cost/low-volume relational sales channels at the end of the axis.

Products generating low revenue per user cannot afford to pay much per user. They should pick low cost channels on the left of the continuum and make profit from volume.

Products with high revenue per user represent a significant cost to the customer. They will need one of the high costs/low volume channels at the right of the continuum. Selling through the strength of the relationship and the services.

DOUG: Can you give an example of both?

ROLAND: For the left of the continuum, imagine your typical free consumer app. It will generate revenue through advertising, a few dollars per year per user at most. This means it cannot spend much to get new users. It should rely on viral acquisition channels like friends inviting friends.

DOUG: At the other end of the spectrum, we can imagine a company selling enterprise software.

ROLAND: Yes, we are talking licenses are worth hundreds of thousands of dollars per year. Of course the enterprise customer only invests such an amount if they expect to make a return. That return will come from significant impact onto one of the business processes. Mapping out that impact requires a long sales cycle and dedicated sales representatives. Sales reps guide buyers through the changes required and help them draw up change plans. They also navigate the decision-makers that will have to buy into the proposal.

4.10   Getting Ready to Raise Series B

DOUG: How many companies raise a series B? How big is it? What do investors expect to see built in return for the investment?

ROLAND: Historically, 61% of tech companies who raised a Series A were also able to raise a series B. The series B investment round represents a giant leap in the funds invested. Seed investments often remain between $500,000 and 1 1/2 million dollars. Series A are often between 2 million and 5 million. But Series B are in the range of $10 million-$50 million.

DOUG: Wow, that is a big jump. Why so large?

ROLAND: There are two reasons.

1. The business is now so de-risked that investors know they have a potential winner on hand. With this knowledge, they have an incentive to gain a larger share. So they invest more.

2. The goal of series B is to blitzscale distribution (sales and marketing). The company needs to occupy the product-market-niche before incumbents catch up. Series B is a giant investment in go-to-market-capacity, whether it represents:

   • hiring tens of salespeople,

- million-dollar marketing budgets,
- building affiliate networks,
- partnering with outside sales channels.

DOUG: Does it have to grow this fast though? Why not build up a sales-force over time? So that it is easier to hire the right people when they are available?

ROLAND: Because of the inherent urgency of scaling. The problem: a "proven" business model is also attractive to would-be competitors. Once the scaleup has a winning market formula, it kicks off a race to occupy that market as fast as possible. Most scaleups fail by letting their market slip to competitors. Not by scaling their go-to-market-capacity too fast. Peter Thiel highlighted this insight in his interview with the *Masters of Scale* podcast (Hoffman, 2017a). He knows of no company that has failed for scaling too quickly. But he knows many that have failed for not scaling quickly enough.

DOUG: Now our freshman scaleup has mastered all these competences. Are they ready for series B?

ROLAND: Yes, they should be. As mentioned before, the purpose of series B is to scale up sales and marketing. To occupy the product-market-niche fast, before the competition does. Here is what the pitch should contain.

Scaling the customer base profitably This is the most important talking point. It comes down to the cost of customer acquisition being lower than the customers' lifetime value.

A true market is developing. Serious competitors are vying over the same market that you are in. In early stages it is common to have a newly developed markets to yourself. But markets at this stage need competition or investors will think something is wrong. Competition is proof of a viable market opportunity. Naturally, investors want that proof before funding the $10-$50 million common for series B.

The buzz the company has attracted. The amount of free promotion it is getting from champions that are not paid by the company. You want to show you have the wind in the back. And that you are on track to become the number one player in this particular market.

DOUG: What things would you recommend funders avoid in their Series B decks?

ROLAND: I recommend not to overstate the number of sandboxes that the company is playing in. Founders love to show the traction the have seen across different verticals. They love to imply that each is a major market opportunity. Series B investors will think of this "thin spread" as a sideshow at best, a major execution risk at worst.

DOUG: Is it better to show that the company is on the way to dominating a few sandboxes?

ROLAND: That is exactly it. And that most of its priorities are to entrench itself deeper into those sandboxes. In other words, show commitment to the perfect product for one small set of sandboxes. Rather than trying to sell a generic product across hundreds of different sandboxes.

Four Decisions™ *Tech Edition* Tools: Strategy Decision

Sandboxes: Defining Competitive Focus over Time

Scale-up Ally
Keep growing, keep your share

1. Define the sandboxes you're currently active in

| Products Sold |
| Geographies Covered |
| Segments Targeted |
| Key Activities Performed In-House *e.g. Research, Dev, Mktg, Sales, Service, Billing* |

2. Plot # of sandboxes per axis and connect dots

3. Mark cells inside the curve: ⬛ strong ◯ weak

4. Define the sandboxes of your key competitors

5. Plot each competitor's curve in a different color

6. As a group, discuss how the curves compare

7. Pick your sandbox conquests battle by battle

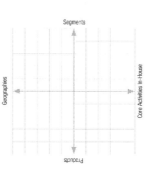

Short-term	Mid-term	Long-term

8. Plot your three target curves in a different color

9. As a group, discuss key short-term actions

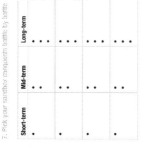
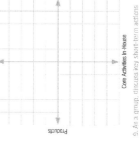

Scale-up Ally Tools v1.1-1.1.2017

Based on IMD Lausanne Growth Strategy models, adapted by Howard Sambelis ©Scale-up Allies, LLC. All Rights Reserved.

Figure 4.7: Worksheet: Sandboxes/Competitive Focus

Sophomore Scaleups: Mastering Deepening

DOUG: We have now reached the stage of the sophomore scaleup. What does a scaleup look like when they have reached the sophomore stage?

ROLAND: We are looking at a company of a tribe-sized team, between 30 and 100 employees. The company has reached solid market-channel-fit, and is reaching customers in ever more verticals. The business model feels like it is "starting to work." New hires work on making the business model more repeatable and scalable.

DOUG: How about financial success?

ROLAND: The scaleup is now optimizing unit profitability *after* marketing/sales. The customer acquisition cost should remain under the expected customer lifetime value.

DOUG: So our sophomore scaleup must have reached quite some critical mass in the market.

ROLAND: Yes, so much that the company's product-market-niche is starting to attract competition. This further validates the market but it also introduces more challenge and risk.

Overall, it feels like the company has the wind in its back. There are plenty of people promoting the company. The PR team is reaching some traction. Investors line up to start funding series B. The key challenge for management is to keep the ship on a steady course. This means delegating their natural affinity for agility downwards into cross-functional teams.

5.1 From Broadening to Deepening

DOUG: You give this chapter the subtitle "Mastering Deepening." Why?

ROLAND: Sophomore scaleups know how to sell and service the early market. Those customers open to new offerings. But the early market represents only one in six potential customers. To sustain their growth, they must break into the mainstream market.

DOUG: If they do not, what happens?

ROLAND: They get stuck in Geoffrey Moore's famous "chasm" (Moore, 2013). Our picture "the sophomore slump" on page 147 shows the risk of growth stopping altogether. The visionary customers leave and the company fails to replace them with new customers from the mainstream market.

DOUG: And that mainstream market requires "deepening?" What do you mean with that?

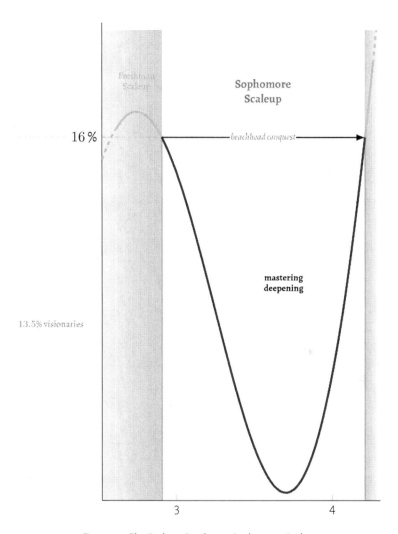

Figure 5.1: The Scaleup Roadmap: Sophomore Scaleups

ROLAND: Think of it as a contrast with "broadening." Freshman scaleups generate growth by adding new verticals, new products and new geographies. Sophomore scaleups that keep this up this broadening tactic tend to implode. There are simply too many complexities caused by serving all these disparate segments.

DOUG: I have seen this happen! So-called startups slowing down so much that they can no longer compete on speed. They tend to die an agonizing death.

ROLAND: Successful sophomore scaleups focus on the few segments with the most traction. They learn to serve customers in that segment ever better and more completely. That is what I mean with deepening.

DOUG: I worked at MacroMedia and Adobe. Both were examples of scaleups narrowing their focus on creative professionals.

ROLAND: I think of Hubspot (Halligan, 2016). They famously built every product to satisfy both "Marketer Mary" and "Owner Ollie." This led to so much compromise that they had to make the hard choice to let go of serving owners. As a result, the more focused product become wildly more successful among marketers.

5.2 Tribe-sized team, Risk of Sycophants

DOUG: The sophomore scaleup has a tribe-sized team now. Anywhere between 30 and 100 people?

ROLAND: That would be a typical size for a sophomore scaleup. With this rapid growth of the workforce, hiring starts to become a real process.

Rather than an incidental activity. Sophomore scaleups often hire their first full-time recruiter.

DOUG: What does this team size mean for how a sophomore scaleup manages their organization?

ROLAND: It is a big challenge to change from an organization of 30 to one of 100 people. All sophomore scaleups start to experience festering management problems right below the surface. This is because how people used to manage before has become ineffective at this larger scale.

DOUG: What management problems are the founders of sophomore scaleups most worried about?

ROLAND: Actually, I often see sophomore scaleups unaware of the management problems they have. Their focus is on making an impact in the markets, and on keeping up momentum to raise the next round. New hires create so much positive energy. It is hard to recognize that there are also problems frustrating people.

DOUG: It must be hard to complain in such a positive work environment?

ROLAND: Nobody wants to be Debbie Downer. Especially since scaleups can have a culture that rewards the biggest cheerleaders. Not those providing the strongest results.

DOUG: That is true, I have seen that happen several times. How come scaleups develop this sycophant syndrome?

ROLAND: It is a function of growing beyond the organization's performance management capacity. The trust-based system does not work beyond 20–30 people.

*"Sophomore scaleups develop sycophant syndrome
when they grow beyond the capacity
of managing performance based on trust"*

ROLAND SIEBELINK

In a freshman scaleup, people work too closely together to need performance metrics. Everyone sees who performs well and who does not. It is easy to nudge someone's performance standards a bit when they do not quite live up to expectations.

DOUG: But a sophomore scaleup grows too big for that performance-management-by-trust?

ROLAND: Exactly. At the scale of a sophomore scaleup, people no longer work personally with everyone else. There is more scope for distrust and parochialism. This is why sophomore scaleups do need their first performance metrics. We will come back to that when we discuss the relentless focus on hiring A-players.

5.3   Trusting Top Team, Peer Accountability

DOUG: One of the new competences you like to see is a trusting top team. Is that building on the trust the founders gained when they were all working in the garage together?

ROLAND: Not anymore. By now, the scaleup will have hired several new executives who did not share that same experience. The original trust between the founders is still there, but it cannot bind the new executives. All scaleups I work with at this stage need a renewal of trust within the entire current team, new and old leaders.

"The original trust between the co-founders cannot bind the newly hired executives"

ROLAND SIEBELINK

DOUG: I can imagine that some teams object to how "touchy-feely" this all sounds. Especially in the face of having to raise a next round.

ROLAND: Only if you try to increase trust when the team members themselves do not see a problem. This is not an exercise to start before the team feels the pain of distrust among their peers. It often manifests itself as a dysfunctional relationship between two or three executives. I often see a CEO forced into a position of constant arbiter between fighting children.

DOUG: What can you do about that situation?

ROLAND: The first step is for teams to admit such a situation is actually dysfunctional. The second step is to make them see that trust between colleagues is crucial. That it lies at the base of any form of collaboration, coordination. Let alone of creation of great things.

DOUG: So how do you deal with trust issues on the team? How can you establish trust between people that have learned to distrust each other?

ROLAND: I find that the key to increasing trust is to see each other as complete human beings. Not just "that nerdy engineer" or "that aggressive sales guy." You can often bring this about with icebreaker exercises at the start of an off-site session.

DOUG: I think you had us tell each other about what kind of teenager we were!

ROLAND: Yes that is a great one. I also ask people to tell each other stories that no one else in the room knows about them. This creates a wave of empathy that can be a first step for creating more trust between people.

DOUG: It cannot just be empathy, can it? You also need complementarity and a shared vision to trust each other?

ROLAND: You are right, we could delve much more deeply into the topic of trust. Which constituent components it has, and how it works like a savings account. But this would move us far beyond the scope of this book.

DOUG: Fair enough. But in summary, what aspects of trust do you focus on in a sophomore scaleup?

ROLAND: In sophomore scaleups, trust is closely linked to accountability. And to clarity about what exactly everyone on the team is going to do to drive the company forwards. That is one of the other competences sophomore scaleups should master. Proper accountability for quarterly rocks. We will talk about that further on in this chapter.

5.4   Scaling Decision-Making

DOUG: At the very outset of this book, you mentioned the ability to delegate decisions. Why is this so important to you?

ROLAND: The ability to scale decision-making is the leading metric to scaling revenues. The more decisions a company can take in parallel, the more constituencies it can serve, the more business it can do and the more revenue it will earn.

> *"If you can scale decision-making,*
> *you can scale revenues"*
>
> ROLAND SIEBELINK

DOUG: Is that not more a matter of increasing the scaleup's workforce?

ROLAND: Unfortunately, it is not that simple. Most scaleups start massive hiring before they have learned to delegate decision-making. You get more people and think you can serve more markets. But you also need a proportional increase in decision delegation. Without it, you will turn the senior management team into a decision-making bottleneck.

DOUG: Am I missing the point here? Is it not up to senior management to make the decision, and for junior people to execute?

ROLAND: I am not talking about big strategic decisions, of course. I mean the many day-to-day decisions that every company needs to make. To answer the many questions and requests from customers that keep business flowing. Let alone from suppliers, fellow employees, partners and other stakeholders.

DOUG: That seems to be a very broad definition of the word "decision." When I think of, say, a call centre agent talking to a customer, I do not think of them taking a decision. All they do is follow a procedure.

ROLAND: In a long-established large company, you would be right. But in a scaleup, that procedure often does not exist yet. Often the process it would be part of (see table 5.1) does not exist yet either. Let alone that top management has already drawn up a policy to guide the process.

Table 5.1: Distinguishing policies, processes and procedures

	Describes	Responsibility	Format
Policy	Company-wide principles	Top mgmt	Sentence
Process	Handovers between departments	Middle mgmt	Flowchart
Procedure	Steps to follow within a department	Frontline mgmt	Checklist

DOUG: I am starting to see the problem... The more new areas the scaleup wants to enter...

ROLAND: ...the more it slows down because of the decision-making bottleneck. Almost regardless of how many people they hire. By default, more new hires just cause new requests to pile up, with a huge bottleneck at the top. Founders get overwhelmed, find delegating even harder, and things fall through the cracks.

5.5 Strengthening Accountability

DOUG: How do you remedy that? Either before the big hiring wave starts or after a scaleup has already hired a bunch of new people?

ROLAND: The first crucial step is to outline functional accountability. By now, the scaleup has enough VPs and Directors to put someone dedicated in charge of each function. The challenge is to move away from the

People: Function Accountability Chart (FACe)

1. Name the person accountable for each function.
2. Ask the four questions at the bottom of the page re: whose name(s) you listed for each function.
3. List Key Performance Indicators (KPIs) for each function.
4. Take your Profit and Loss (P&L), Balance Sheet, and Cash Flow accounting statements and assign a person to each line item, then derive appropriate Results/Outcomes for each function.

Functions	1 Person Accountable	3 Leading Indicators (Key Performance Indicators)	4 Results/Outcomes (P/L or B/S items)
Head of Company			
Marketing			
R&D/Innovation			
Sales			
Operations			
Treasury			
Controller			
Information Technology			
Human Resources			
Talent Development/Learning			
Customer Advocacy			
Heads of Business Units			
• _____			
• _____			
• _____			
• _____			

2. **Identify: 1.** More than 1 person in a seat; **2.** Person in more than 1 seat; **3.** Empty seats; **4.** Enthusiastically rehire?

Gazelles Growth Tools™ v3.3 – 10.1.14 [ENG] For use by Gazelles International Coaches. ©2015 Gazelles, Inc.

For assistance, contact us at coaches@GICoaches.com P-3

Figure 5.2: Gazelles Functional Accountability Chart

founder/CEO directing everyone's day-to-day assignments. Instead, I like to see a peer-accountable team at the top of the organization. One where everyone knows which team member is responsible exactly for what.

DOUG: Is that it? That seems pretty basic.

ROLAND: Does it not? Yet I still have to encounter the first freshman scaleup that had it. That had mastered functional accountability all by itself. The typical applicant scaleup has 1–2 founders making every tactical, day-to-day decisions.

DOUG: Now it scales and scales...

ROLAND: ...and becomes first a freshman scaleup, then a sophomore scaleup. They hire many new VPs. And yet old habits persist. More often than not, these new hires are executives only in name. They have a title, but very little clarity on exactly what that title means. No idea what responsibility it entails, and what success looks like. Hence these team members almost never have a plan for their functional area, as Gerber (2004) recommends every new hire should get.

DOUG: That is shocking. You mean, they have hired all these VPs, and then never told them what to do?

ROLAND: It is easy to see why that would happen if you understand where they are coming from.

In the previous stage, this business was a bootstrapped startup. Think two or three cofounders in a garage. This founding team did everything together–including discussing every decision.

They may have assigned themselves titles like CEO, CTO and CMO. But in reality they were managing the startup as a joint project. Collaboration rested on trust and long-term friendship.

DOUG: Trust they do not necessarily have with new hires.

ROLAND: Exactly. Now that the business has grown, founders have promoted or hired people to manage areas for them. But they do not trust them as much as their cofounders yet. And they also want to remain agile. So typically they fail to give executives a scorecard to just run with. In stead, they give them lots of tactical assignments. And then they evaluate them based on how quickly they can jump.

DOUG: How do you help these teams reach some semblance of real accountability?

ROLAND: Gazelles International Coaches, of which I am part, have developed a Functional Accountability Chart (see page 155) (Gazelles, 2015b). I find this very effective in sharpening functional accountability with a team. With Collins (2001), it emphasizes getting the right people into the right seats.

With the exercise, it becomes obvious how different people interpret each other's responsibilities. No wonder most teams suffer from constant back-and-forth about who does what. Let alone whether their colleagues are doing a good job or a bad one.

DOUG: What parts of functional accountability does the tool cover?

ROLAND: It has three key features:

The right seats The first feature is that the tool defines the "right seats." These seats are independent of the specific titles people in the client company may have.

Single-name boxes The second feature is that it expects a single name in each box. Usually the team will find some names appear in several locations, and other names in none. This needs clearing up.

Leading and lagging metrics The third feature is that it allows two sets of metrics. The leading metric is about the key activity of the function, e.g. meetings held or widgets produced. The lagging metric is for the outcome/result of the function: revenue, gross margin, profit etc.

From the sophomore stage, every scaleup needs a completed Functional Accountability chart. Every team should complete chart with its executive team. And keep it updated once a quarter. It will them diagnose people and performance gaps on the leadership team.

DOUG: Assuming we have sorted that functional accountability out, what is the second step?

ROLAND: Agreeing on the results each function should produce (lagging metric). And what the key activity is that we want each function to perform to get to that number (leading metric). Setting these metrics creates more autonomy for each of the functional leaders.

DOUG: With that, all accountability should be clear!

ROLAND: Actually, we also want to address process accountability. On top of functional accountability. This means that I like to see one executive each in charge of the four "machines" or success formulas:

- Innovation Machine

- Acquisition Machine

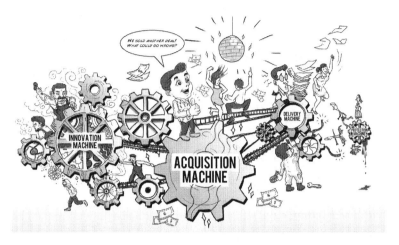

Figure 5.3: The Four Success Formulas of a Scaleup

- Delivery Machine

- Protection Machine (or Resilience Machine).

Each will have lagging metrics (e.g. production and cost per issue) and a leading metric (e.g. % first time right).

5.6   On a Disciplined Quarterly Rhythm

DOUG: You also expect sophomore scaleups to adopt a quarterly rhythm.

ROLAND: Yes, this is a best practice from the Gazelles International Coaches organization. I find it highly applicable to tech scaleups.

1. **The executive team is healthy and aligned.**
   - Team members understand each other's differences, priorities, and styles.
   - The team meets frequently (weekly is best) for strategic thinking.
   - The team participates in ongoing executive education (monthly recommended).
   - The team is able to engage in constructive debates and all members feel comfortable participating.

2. **Everyone is aligned with the #1 thing that needs to be accomplished this quarter to move the company forward.**
   - The Critical Number is identified to move the company ahead this quarter.
   - 3-5 Priorities (Rocks) that support the Critical Number are identified and ranked for the quarter.
   - A Quarterly Theme and Celebration/Reward are announced to all employees that bring the Critical Number to life.
   - Quarterly Theme/Critical Number posted throughout the company and employees are aware of the progress each week.

3. **Communication rhythm is established and information moves through organization accurately and quickly.**
   - All employees are in a daily huddle that lasts less than 15 minutes.
   - All teams have a weekly meeting.
   - The executive and middle managers meet for a day of learning, resolving big issues, and DNA transfer each month.
   - Quarterly and annually, the executive and middle managers meet offsite to work on the 4 Decisions.

4. **Every facet of the organization has a person assigned with accountability for ensuring goals are met.**
   - The Function Accountability Chart (FACe) is completed (right people, doing the right things, right).
   - Financial statements have a person assigned to each line item.
   - Each of the 4-9 processes on the Process Accountability Chart (PACe) has someone that is accountable for them.
   - Each 3-5 year Key Thrust/Capability has a corresponding expert on the Advisory Board if internal expertise doesn't exist.

5. **Ongoing employee input is collected to identify obstacles and opportunities.**
   - All executives (and middle managers) have a Start/Stop/Keep conversation with at least one employee weekly.
   - The insights from employee conversations are shared at the weekly executive team meeting.
   - Employee input about obstacles and opportunities is being collected weekly.
   - A mid-management team is responsible for the process of closing the loop on all obstacles and opportunities.

6. **Reporting and analysis of customer feedback data is as frequent and accurate as financial data.**
   - All executives (and middle managers) have a 4Q conversation with at least one end user weekly.
   - The insights from customer conversations are shared at the weekly executive team meeting.
   - All employees are involved in collecting customer data.
   - A mid-management team is responsible for the process of closing the loop on all customer feedback.

7. **Core Values and Purpose are "alive" in the organization.**
   - Core Values are discovered, Purpose is articulated, and both are known by all employees.
   - All executives and middle managers refer back to the Core Values and Purpose when giving praise or reprimands.
   - HR processes and activities align with the Core Values and Purpose (hiring, orientation, appraisal, recognition, etc.).
   - Actions are identified and implemented each quarter to strengthen the Core Values and Purpose in the organization.

8. **Employees can articulate the following key components of the company's strategy accurately.**
   - Big Hairy Audacious Goal (BHAG®) — progress is tracked and visible.
   - Core Customer(s) — their profile in 25 words or less.
   - 3 Brand Promises — and the corresponding Brand Promise KPIs reported on weekly.
   - Elevator Pitch — a compelling response to the question "What does your company do?"

9. **All employees can answer quantitatively whether they had a good day or week (column 7 of the One-Page Strategic Plan).**
   - 1 or 2 Key Performance Indicators (KPIs) are reported on weekly for each role/person.
   - Each employee has 1 Critical Number that aligns with the company's Critical Number for the quarter (clear line of sight).
   - Each individual/team has 3-5 Quarterly Priorities/Rocks that align with those of the company.
   - All executives and middle managers have a coach (or peer coach) holding them accountable to behavior changes.

10. **The company's plans and performance are visible to everyone.**
    - A "situation room" is established for weekly meetings (physical or virtual).
    - Core Values, Purpose and Priorities are posted throughout the company.
    - Scoreboards are up everywhere displaying current progress on KPIs and Critical Numbers.
    - There is a system in place for tracking and managing the cascading Priorities and KPIs.

Figure 5.4: Gazelles Checklist: Rockefeller Habits™

It means nothing more than that the top team has a quarterly thinking and planning session. They use this to set joint priorities for the next quarter.

DOUG: How is that new? All executive teams I know already do these off-sites.

ROLAND: They do, but it is not the input that matters. It is the output. The usual off-sites rarely create real consensus about the state of the company. Let alone what the priorities should be for the next quarter.

DOUG: Then how can you tell if a sophomore scaleup has really mastered the quarterly rhythm?

ROLAND: My key checkpoints are that the company (1) has a completed One-Page-Strategic-Plan in use and (2) sets new priorities only in the quarterly off-site sessions. In other words, sophomore scaleups are learning to let go of the extremes of founder agility. Of the feeling that there is a new corporate priority every week.

DOUG: What if the environment changes and a new priority comes into existence?

ROLAND: Of course leaders should still bring up new ideas throughout the quarter. But the company should have the reflex to set a new priority only in the next quarterly planning session. This creates the calm for people to execute on their targets and deliver real results. Rather than having to restart something you all the time.

DOUG: Are there any rules to how to conduct the quarterly planning session itself?

see Susko, Shannon

Table 5.2: Ten Commandments for Effective Planning Offsites

Rule	Topic	Best practice
#1	Fixed dates	Set up planning sessions as repeating events like "the last Friday of each quarter" so that people get into a fixed rhythm.
#2	One method	Pick one solid framework to guide your strategy and execution, such as "Scaling Up". Do not focus each session on a new framework.
#3	Use a diagnostic	Find some way of scoring yourselves on progress, e.g. the Rockefeller Habits survey or the 4D Assessment.
#4	Gather input	Ask customers and employees what the scaleup should stop, start and keep doing. Also ask middle managers for their SWOT analysis.
#5	Prepare thoughts	Let participants gather their thoughts before the workshop by sending everyone reading material and a preparation worksheet.
#6	Cross-functional	Do not structure the agenda around reviewing every function. Instead, focus it on the outputs of the scaleup at large, visible to external stakeholders.
#7	Forward-looking	Spend no more than 20–25% of the time on reviewing the last quarter. Identify key issues and move on to planning to resolve them.
#8	Thought-provoking	Add exercises designed to expand participants' thinking, especially when focused on a blind spot the scaleup team may have.
#9	External facilitator	Find a coach or facilitator from outside the company to lead the session. Let the CEO sit back, observe their team and focus on the content.
#10	Preframed output	Be clear upfront what output the team will have produced coming out of the session. E.g. a One-Page-Strategic-Plan with five Quarterly Rocks.

ROLAND: There are many rules and best practices. We have summarized ten of them in table 5.2.

DOUG: Excellent! Let me touch on a few of them. Rule #3 is to use diagnostics.

ROLAND: The team should use an unbiased diagnostic tool to get a sense for how the company is doing. I recommend Gazelles *Rockefeller Habits* (Gazelles, 2015a) or the *20 Scaleup Levers* available on our website. Most companies using these diagnostic tools have found them invaluable. They help to discover blind spots they had no other way of knowing about.

DOUG: I notice rule #6 is to focus on the company at large.

ROLAND: Absolutely, as opposed to functions and departments. One of the best ways to make a quarterly off-site ineffective is to review of each function's quarterly results. The focus needs to be on the team managing the company at large, not on each executive managing each function.

DOUG: Rule #7 is not to dwell on past results.

ROLAND: I advocate limiting the review of the last quarter to just an hour or two. You should focus the bulk of the session on new learning. And on strong alignment around new quarterly goals for the entire company.

DOUG: You look to fill a planning session with thought-provoking exercises.

ROLAND: Yes, the planning session should contain exercises that help expand the team's thinking. For example in all working through the same one-page tools. This is far superior to executives all bringing in their own presentation decks. Or to open discussion without any structure.

DOUG: As a ninth rule, you do not want the CEO to lead the workshop.

Strategy: Strengths, Weaknesses, Trends (SWT)

Gazelles
GROWING LEADERS-GROWING COMPANIES

Trends

What are the significant changes in technology, distribution, product innovation, markets, consumer, and social trends around the world that might impact your industry and organization?

Strengths/Core Competencies	Weaknesses
What are the inherent strengths of the organization that have been the source of your success?	What are the inherent weaknesses of the organization that aren't likely to change?

Figure 5.5: Gazelles Worksheet: Strengths-Weaknesses-Trends

Four Decisions™ Tech Edition Tools: Execution Decision
Preparing for a Quarterly Planning Session

Quarter evaluation   *Please read "we"/"us" as the business/unit at large, not just your own function*

Note: this worksheet is meant for the personal preparation of participants. Info not collected in advance.

1. What business aspects have been going well this quarter? What results can we all be proud of?

2. What business aspects have been disappointing this quarter? Where do we all need improvement?

3. How has cooperation with our peers been this quarter? What has worked well, what not?

4. What persistent issue(s) have we been ignoring and/or been unable to solve this quarter?

Accountability update

5. Do you see your current function as one coherent role or are you really fulfilling multiple roles?
Rule of thumb: if you could imagine hiring someone to do one part of your job, that's a separate role.

Role #1: your key role   **Role #2: (optional)**   **Role #3: (optional)**

6. What, in a Tweet-sized sentence, is the main current mission of each role you fulfil?
E.g. for a scaleup CEO: "to bring the company to a successful IPO"

7. What are the max. 5 functional accountabilities of each role you fulfil?

8. What is *the most* critical number (metric) to improve on for each role you fulfil, for next quarter?

One-Page Strategic Plan Update Preparation and Rock Brainstorming

9. Review our One-Page Strategic Plan for the quarter. Which elements need what update?

a. Strengths/Weaknesses/Trends

b. Core values

c. Purpose

d. Economic engine & BHAG

e. Brand Promises & Brand Promise KPIs

f. Key thrusts and capabilities, sandbox

g. Financial targets (3y and/or 1y)

h. Annual critical numbers/key initiatives

i. Other

10. Based on all of the above, what 3-5 rocks do you think we should work on next quarter?

Figure 5.6: Worksheet: Planning Session Preparation

ROLAND: Correct. A founder/CEO leading the workshop immediately sets up their team for failure. It prevents them from engaging in real discussion and bringing up sensitive issues.

Far better to hire an external moderator or coach, who can allow the leader to sit back. The CEO can now observe their people discuss the business, and learn from their insights. Without having the personal responsibility to drive to planning session forward.

5.7 Mastering Rock Delivery

DOUG: You mentioned that scaling decision-making depends on rock delivery. What is rock delivery?

ROLAND: A "rock" is the term we use for a quarterly priority. It comes from the "rocks in a jar" story that Stephen Covey made famous. (Covey, 2013) Rock accountability simply means delivering on priorities. I want sophomore scaleups to master delivering cross-functional priorities with high reliability. That means:

- assigning an owner to each of the rocks

- defining key streams or set milestones that help illustrate how to execute the rock

- setting a metric to check the success of the rock.

DOUG: So first the scaleup has to set cross-functional priorities?

ROLAND: That is correct. As the business grows, demands on it keep increasing. People feel torn in all directions. The only way to set real

Scale-up Ally
keep growing, keep your culture

Planning Session: Tracking Candidate Priorities Across Exercises

Appropriate time horizon
- LT/3yr: new capability thrust
- MT/1y: program, 2+ proj
- ST/1q: tangible project

Exercises/Discussions

Date/time	Theme/Title of Exercise	My key insight(s) from this discussion	Outcome: top team priority(ies)

Figure 5.7: Worksheet: Candidate Priorities

priorities is across the organization. Rather than function-by-function, as so many organizations tend to do.

It is not only the cross-functionality that matters. It is also the ability to limit oneself to a workable list. And to use time boxing to make sure each priority has a deadline.

DOUG: In this context, what exactly do you mean with a priority?

ROLAND: I define a priority as an area where the business wants to spend extra management effort. Not only an important metric to keep track of, but one that you want to make significant improvement on. As Gazelles coaches, we help clients sets priorities for three horizons in succession:

- three year (longer-term) capabilities

- annual (midterm) objectives

- quarterly rocks.

We insist the team design each to really move the needle for the company. The horizons are to recognize that different projects take different amounts of time. Building up a a new capability will last several years. A major strategic goal can be achievable in one year. And a key technical change can often take place within a quarter.

DOUG: How do you recommend a sophomore scaleup approach setting all these priorities?

ROLAND: I can think of five key levers.

Priorities as key output First, these priorities should be the key output of any executive offsite. Executive teams always organize offsites

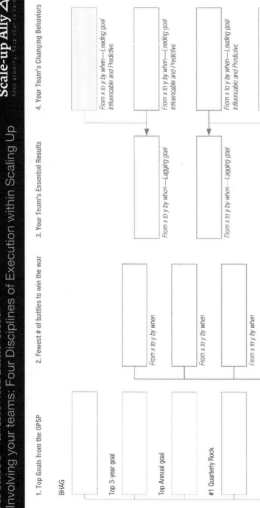

Figure 5.8: Worksheet: Involving Your Team

for themselves. But they rarely structure them around delivering a clear outcome. If the executive off-site does not produce priorities, it is a failure.

Build on core decision consensus Second, in my experience, the team needs to start from consensus on some core decisions. Like core values, core purpose and the economic engine. It is only when they agree on these fundamentals that they can come to see the same priorities. That is why embracing the core identity is a key competence that I expect a freshman scaleup to master.

Agreed on a three year unit target Third, the team should agree on their (financial and) unit target for three years out. Not only the numbers, but also what new competences, products etc. it will need to reach those numbers. Shannon Byrne Susko (2018) has perfected this process with the *3-Year Highly Achievable Goal* (3HAG)*see* 3HAG.

From long term to short term Fourth, the team should follow the right cadence from long term to short term. It needs agreement on three year capabilities before deciding on annual objectives. It should set its annual objectives before updating its quarterly rocks.

Guided by external facilitator Finally, discussion quality often benefits when an external facilitator guides the debate. Without a facilitator, the CEO feels compelled to lead the discussion. A facilitator's neutral role lets the CEO sit back and take part like everyone else. This encourages people saying what they really think—not what they think the CEO wants them to say. More often than not, this leads to surprising new insights that represent genuine breakthroughs for the team.

DOUG: Hold on, you mentioned each rock is a cross-functional quarterly priority. Then how do you assign rock to one of the functional heads present in the meeting?

ROLAND: Good observation. At this stage, sophomore scaleups learn to stop equating an executive completely with their function.

Let's say you have a rock to improve customer feedback systems. For example by instituting a net promoter system. You may not have a typical owner for this rock, a head of customer advocacy.

Less evolved teams will expect the founder/CEO to be accountable, for lack of a functional owner. More evolved teams will find anyone with experience in or even just passion for this project. And assign it to that person regardless of their functional responsibility.

> *"Encourage people volunteering for deliverables outside their immediate functional responsibility."*

ROLAND SIEBELINK

DOUG: That needs much trust, for someone on a team to get authority to take all the decisions.

ROLAND: The remit is a little bit more restricted. You can rely much more on the team delivering results if each rock has a clear owner. But that does not imply that each owner can take all decisions by themselves.

What it does imply, is that the owner has a responsibility to seek feedback from all other relevant stakeholders. And then they can take a decision by taking the bulk of that feedback into account. It is about making sure people get heard, not about ensuring everybody gets their way.

Figure 5.9: Letting each rock owner deliver on behalf of the team

5.8 Breaking into Mainstream Markets

DOUG: To continue growing, the sophomore scaleup needs to "master deepening." That also implies a change of customers?

ROLAND: Yes, and this is a crucial point to master for a sophomore scaleup. The scaleup must move away from serving a plethora of visionary early-adopters. Instead, it has to conquer its first mainstream pragmatists.

DOUG: Why, if they have had such big market success with the early adopters?

ROLAND: I often get this question. It has to do with Founder-CEOs liking their early adopter customers so much. But the reasons are simple:

1. There are not enough early adopters around to keep up the expected growth rates.

2. Early adopters signed up for you when you were cool and new. And for that same reason, they will soon move away to an even newer and cooler competitor.

DOUG: They are like a burning platform.

ROLAND: Exactly. Early Adopters do not last. You can only build a lasting franchise with mainstream customers. Starting with the early majority: our pragmatists.

DOUG: What is so different about marketing to pragmatists?

ROLAND: Moore (2013, Chapter 2) has provided excellent descriptions and detail about mainstream customers. I could not do them justice. But to highlight some of his main points:

- Early majority customers want to avoid risk. Contrast this with early *adopter* customers who want to capture an opportunity.

- Early majority customers want to wait until the product works completely. They also want it bundled with everything you need ("the whole product").

- Early majority customers like to see that there is enough competition in the market. No competition means the market is not validated yet. But they also like to see your offering is number one.

- They want to see an ecosystem for support and aftermarket supplies, to keep low total cost of ownership.

- Above all, they want to see references from mainstream customers like themselves. Especially from within their own vertical or industry.

DOUG: That is a bit of a Catch–22, is it not? That you *need* mainstream customers to *get* mainstream customers?

> *"Visionaries, as a group, make a*
> *very poor reference base for pragmatists."*
>
> GEOFFREY MOORE

ROLAND: You are spot on. That circularity is the key point Moore (2013) made with *Crossing the Chasm*. Mainstream customers do not buy based on recommendations of early adopter customers. Only from mainstream customers like themselves, in their own industry.

DOUG: How is a sophomore scaleup supposed to break through that conundrum?

ROLAND: I cannot do justice here to the detailed action plan that Moore (2013) provides. Founders should definitely read his book. But the key recommendation is to stop spreading resources across many verticals. To pick one beachhead in the mainstream where, with massive resources, you become number one within a year.

5.9 Developing the Whole Product

DOUG: That is intriguing. Sophomore scaleups should get their growth from fewer industries rather than more? That seems counterintuitive.

ROLAND: Counterintuitive indeed. This is why so many scaleups fail at this stage. The founders find it too risky to prefer one vertical over another. They feel growth should come from expansion and so they spread resources too thin.

DOUG: Toeholds in several verticals are a way of mitigation risk, are they not?

ROLAND: But apply the technology adoption cycle, and you see the huge concentration of risk. Because every toehold, every vertical, represents only early adopters. Only founders of the visionaries' volatility find courage to make these painful choices.

DOUG: How certain is it that scaleups serve only visionaries across these verticals? I should think it is possible that they have many mainstream customers too.

ROLAND: This is a great question, and it comes to the heart of the problem in crossing the chasm. I will predict that any sophomore scaleup serving

"Any sophomore scaleup serving more than two verticals is missing the mainstream market"

ROLAND SIEBELINK

three or more verticals is missing the mainstream market. They are stuck in the early-adopter (visionaries) segment.

DOUG: How can you be so sure?

ROLAND: Because a scaleup has only a few hundred employees. And there is only one way to serve several verticals with limited resources. Without disrespect to the founders: with a lowest common denominator product.

DOUG: You mean a product that offers only the features that all verticals want? Nothing specific for any particular vertical?

"There is only one way to serve several verticals with limited resources: with a lowest common denominator product."

ROLAND SIEBELINK

ROLAND: Yes, that is exactly what I mean. It is what Moore calls the 80% product, the one that has the core technology and can serve many use cases. But where the user themselves has to make up or work around the remaining 20%. For example:

- integrating with systems standard in the vertical;

- features reflecting specific idiosyncrasies of the vertical, etc.

- distribution through channels common in the vertical;

- full support from ecosystem partners focused on the vertical.

DOUG: The 20% that visionaries skip, but that mainstream customers care about.

ROLAND: Exactly. The desire to sell into several verticals leads to focusing on economies of scope. To a "one size fits all" product. One that visionaries can be happy enough with. But that pragmatists experience as incomplete. The remaining 20% of the "100% product" is disparate between verticals. So I can predict with near certainty that a scaleup with limited resources only sells the 80% product. And that it will not have penetrated the mainstream market.

DOUG: How do you recommend a scaleup chooses its mainstream beach-head?

ROLAND: Moore (2013) has a great outline of this consensus-building process. It helps teams move from a long list of ideas, a short list of investigable options, to the one pick that stands out most. All with clear criteria which beachhead is most likely to bring the company success.

In my own planning sessions, we use the worksheet in figure 5.10 that contains the essence of Moore's process. This helps teams that want to get to an initial hypothesis with only an hour or two to spend.

Crossing the Chasm: Targeting a Beachhead Segment

Scale-up Ally △
keep growing. keep your culture.

1. Individually, identify target customer characters

2. Individually, score (1..5) to weed out potential showstoppers

3. Individually, score (1..5) top passes from previous question on nice-to-have factors

Identifiable economic buyers—within one word-of-mouth market

Industry	Geography	Job title		TgtCust **Compelling reason to buy**			**Pass?**		**Factors increasing chances of success**						**Our one choice**
				Access	Pain &	Whole	No com-	Top X	Partners/	Sales	Price/	Cred-	Bowling		
				Econ.byr.	Anxiety	Prod/3m	petition	w/o lows	allies	channel	value	bility	Pins		choice

4. Describe your chosen beachhead segment in full

Buyers (Ec, Tc, EU)	Job to be done	Current pain point	New solution	Econ. rewards	Whole Product	Partners/Allies	Sales Channel	Pricing	Geo calibration
									___ % of our V___ sales=
									___ % tgt mkt share =
									Target geography=

Figure 5.10: Worksheet: Targeting a Beachhead

5.10   Playing in Fewer Sandboxes

DOUG: "Playing in fewer sandboxes"—what a funny title. How do you use this metaphor for scaleups?

ROLAND: The sandbox is a field of play. It is a target market or focus area. It encompasses the type of customer, a type of product and a geographical region.

DOUG: That sounds quite abstract. Can you give us an example of a sandbox?

ROLAND: Sorry, yes, some examples may help to illustrate the concept better. Imagine a sophomore scaleup in enterprise software. Their focus area or sandbox could be:

- business rules management software (product)

- for government organizations (customer)

- in North America (geography).

DOUG: What if they also serve healthcare companies?

ROLAND: That would constitute a second sandbox. The sandboxes are the number of combinations. The permutations between the product, the customer and the geographic dimension.

DOUG: So if they started targeting customers in EMEA too, this would double the number of sandboxes?

ROLAND: Correct. Assuming it still has one product, our scaleup would play in four sandboxes:

1. Government organizations in North-America

2. Healthcare organizations in North-America

3. Government organizations in EMEA

4. Healthcare organizations in EMEA

DOUG: And then if it added another product, the number of sandboxes would double to eight?

ROLAND: Correct again. Assuming it would sell the new product to both segments in both geographies, of course.

DOUG: But then what do you mean with sandbox discipline?

ROLAND: Here is the problem. Startups and freshman scaleups build sales wherever they find a customer. By the time they reach sophomore stage, they often have:

- a few customers each in three or four verticals

- tried to launch a second and maybe third product,

- started business in Europe

- maybe closed a partnership deal in Asia or Australia

This makes them active in far more sandboxes than they have realistic resources for. As a result, it is very common to see not a single sandbox that they are close to dominating.

DOUG: They are spreading themselves too thin.

ROLAND: That is exactly right. The key competence I want sophomore scaleups to master is to occupy as few sandboxes as possible.

Figure 5.11: Jumping into New Sandboxes Prematurely

1. Teams need to be aware of the sheer number of sandboxes you
   have already dipped your toe into. Teams are often shocked to
   find they cover over 100 sandboxes. Especially when they start
   comparing themselves to more disciplined competitors.

2. They need to analyze waterfall charts on which sandboxes generate
   profits. And which only losses. Revenue-wise, all sandboxes look
   attractive. But profit-wise, you often see one or two sandboxes
   subsidizing tens of others. Video advertising startup Zentrick had
   to tackle this challenge in the startup stage already. As CTO Pieter
   Mees related, even reducing from three to two business lines had
   a massive effect (Siebelink, 2017a).

181

3. The team needs to focus most resources on the most profitable sandboxes. And to retreat from the most loss-making sandboxes.

DOUG: Does that mean they have to call a loss in the sandboxes that they could not make work?

ROLAND: It does not have to be a public retreat. I am looking for the discipline of not throwing good money after bad. That the scaleup focus resources not on sandboxes where it is weakest, but on where it is strongest. That it not invest in areas where it lacks key competences or the market position to compete.

DOUG: I definitely experienced this syndrome of spreading ourselves too thin in many of the scaleups I worked at.

ROLAND: It is very common indeed. Instead, I like to see a sophomore focusing resources on the few sandboxes that it has a real chance to dominate. And to keep other sandboxes open at most as options, at minimal funding levels.

DOUG: Fewer sandboxes would also help to reduce confusion.

ROLAND: Absolutely, good point! Confusion stems from vague decisions. From senior managers failing to take the hard decisions and to communicate clearly. This happens when executives optimize their decisions for consensus rather than for clarity. By mixing opposing perspectives, they decide nothing real. Instead, they delegate the problem to the lower levels that most definitely cannot solve it. The best remedy is to force clarity unto executive decisions and policies:

1. Teach and follow *one* standard issue resolution method:

Rapid Issue Resolution Process

Scale-up Ally △
Keep growing. Keep your culture.

1. Problem/issue to be solved
Reporter: summarize what is the problem you are trying to solve

2. Priority on issue list
Team: prioritize full list first

☐ Top 3 issue: solve now
☐ Not top 3: defer solving

3a. Initial owner, need not be reporter
Role: gather input, prepare proposed solution

3b. Challenge, need not be reporter
Role: review with owner, broaden solution set

4. What is the real issue here? The root cause?
Owner/challenger: dig deeper, use the "five whys" to find the root

5. What alternatives could solve the root cause?
Owner/challenger: prepare at least three alternative solutions

6a. As a team, decide on the simplest solution
Team: **taking a decision** beats ~~waiting for consensus~~

6b. Transfer to action items list
Owner of the key action item (need not be initial owner):

Deadline to implement (default: one week after decision)

Scale-Up Ally Tools v2.0 c1.2018

Source: Rocket Scientists after RISO, Karen Morris, Gino Wickman, All Rights Reserved

Trademark ©2018 Scale-up Allies LLC . All Rights Reserved

Figure 5.12: Worksheet: Rapid Issue Resolution

- Plan, Do, Study, Adjust

- Identify, Discuss and Solve

- Define, Measure, Analyze, Improve and Control

- Or any other *one* method you find useful. Just do not combine and confuse.

2. Listen to opinions of all concerned before formulating a solution;

3. Ensure consent to a Tweet-sized written version that...

4. ...you will communicate to the broader company.

In my experience, writing down your decisions irons out 90% of the "waffle" before the rest of the organization has a chance to get confused.

5.11   Delegating Agility

DOUG: You mentioned that sophomore scaleups often have a challenge with delegating agility. What do you mean with that?

ROLAND: Sophomore scaleups start hiring more and more people. Soon it becomes impossible for the founders to keep track of everything that is going on. Of every request coming in. To ensure all employees can perform to the best of their abilities, they need to have a solid base to work from.

DOUG: What does that mean, what do employees need to know?

ROLAND: Just a few "leverage decisions"—decisions on which most other tactical decisions can be based:

- which customers the company is targeting and which not;

- what products the company is selling and what not;

- how the company differentiates itself from competitors;

- on which attributes it would rather not compete, etc.

> *"Anyone with children will recognize*
> *the fundamentals [...] as*
> *(1) Have a handful of rules*
> *(2) Repeat yourself a lot*
> *(3) Act consistently with those rules"*

VERNE HARNISH

DOUG: That does not sound like delegating agility, quite the opposite! It sounds like imposing strict guidelines.

ROLAND: That is the exact paradox. As you scale, you want tens or hundreds of employee teams to develop agile solutions in their own right. But you also want all these solutions to fit together in a coherent whole. The only way you can achieve both is to establish stable guardrails.

DOUG: But what about staying agile? These commitments would make it much harder to change course.

ROLAND: Exactly. And that is fully intended. Let me explain. In previous stages, all successful founders have learned to be very agile. They have grown comfortable with pivoting to a new approach at the first sign of trouble. This competence is crucial while you are a startup, still looking for product-market-fit.

DOUG: But it becomes less important after product-market-fit?

ROLAND: When you run a larger ship, changing course for every minor wave would destroy all momentum. It is only when you set a clear course that your teams can focus all their efforts in one direction. They can try different tactics, learn from experience, and drive higher performance. They can take full accountability over each crucial part of your ship. They will soon be better at managing that part of the ship than you could have ever been yourself. You are now hiring smart people who can tell you what to do.

"On a ship constantly changing course,
even large crews can do nothing
but wait for the next command."

ROLAND SIEBELINK

DOUG: Most founders I know would rather put off key strategic choices like customer, value proposition and differentiation.

ROLAND: True, and this is more than appropriate in the startup phase. But it is a delegation of uncertainty in the scaleup phase. By keeping all options open, you guarantee that no option will come true. On a ship constantly changing course, employees can only wait for the next command from above. There is no point trying out different things and learning from experience. No point in giving their best. You may be

186

hiring smart people, but you still have to tell them what to do every day. What is the point of that?

> *"Successful firms [...simultaneously maintain...]*
> *bottom-up internal experimentation [...]*
> *and top-driven strategic intent."*

ROBERT A. BURGELMAN

DOUG: You are saying that a scaleup should de-emphasize agility over stability?

ROLAND: I am saying that founders should delegate the agility to their teams. Founders should teach their skills in agile experimentation to all lower level teams. Let the build-measure-learn cycles take place in many frontline teams in parallel. Let these teams use build-measure learn to figure out faster innovation. To drive more efficient marketing, shorter sales cycles, higher customer satisfaction, all that.

DOUG: Does this also help to reduce the friction that we typically see growing in sophomore scaleups?

ROLAND: Friction stems from unclear roles. From management telling teams to work together, without telling them who does what. There is a very easy way to avoid this for the most important processes:

1. Outline your core processes as per the previous chapter.

2. Ensure all senior managers consent that this is how everything should work.

3. Then bundle them together and name them something like "The [your company] way." (Wickman, 2013)

If you keep the processes simple enough, they will help avoid much bureaucracy.

DOUG: In a sophomore scaleup, agility is no longer appropriate.

ROLAND: Exactly. At least not in the core decisions and at the top. The ship has become too big for that. What it needs now is for the top team to become firm about its strategic intent. For the top team to set a course of "leverage decisions" that the ship can follow for a long time. In the face of different weather patterns, enemy ships, fishing grounds, whatever the ship may encounter. The more the top can keep these leverage decisions constant, the more the frontline can think long-term. The more they will use all their creativity to do better and better at providing value to the company.

DOUG: So you are saying: agile at the bottom, rigid at the top?

ROLAND: That is a bit harsh. Day-to-day agility and constant pivoting should now take place at the front of the organization. In parallel streams of experimentation and continuous improvement. At the top of the organization, I try to teach executives to be long-term agile. To embrace some core identity decisions about things that will never change, to set longer-term goals. And then to be flexible and adaptable about the shorter-term goals that help to reach them.

5.12   Ticking the Boxes for Series C

DOUG: When is a sophomore scaleup ready to raise their Series C?

Four Decisions™ *Tech Edition* Tools: Cash Decision

Cash Acceleration/Improving your Success Formulas

Scale-up Ally
Keep growing. Keep your culture.

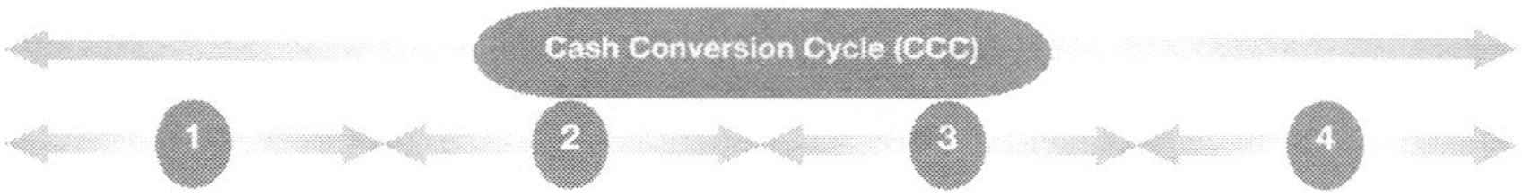

Cash Conversion Cycle (CCC)
1
2
3
4

	Product Development Cycle Innovation Formula	Marketing & Sales Cycle Customer-Attraction Formula	Customer Success Cycle Value Delivery Formula	Billing & Payment Profit Protection Formula	Aggregate Total
***d* Cycle time**					
Ways to Improve					
% 1st time right					
Ways to Improve					
$€¥£₣ Cost					
Ways to Improve					

Scale-Up Ally Tools v1.2-08.2017

After MOORE (G.A.) 2013. *Crossing the Chasm, 3rd Edition*. All right reserved.

Figure 5.13: Worksheet: Cash Acceleration

Quarterly Rock: Preparing for Successful Execution

Scale-up Ally △
keep growing. keep your culture

1. Quarterly Rock Name

2. Sponsoring Executive

3. Quarterly Rock Leader and Team Members

Name	Department	Office

4. Overall Deliverable—Sponsor considers this rock done when . . .

5. Requirements for this Rock to succeed (budget, time, resources; discuss with your Sponsor)

6. Breakdown of overall deliverable; key milestones on the way to the Rock's success

#	Milestone/Subproject/Epic	By when (date)	Owner
1			
2			
3			
4			
5			

7. Risks that might imperil this Rock's success (ask the Sponsor to help you manage these)

8. Next steps to "hit the ground running" with this Rock from next week

#	What	By when (date)	Who
1			
2			
3			
4			
5			
6			

Figure 5.14: Worksheet: Quarterly Rock Execution

ROLAND: The purpose of Series C is to entrench the dominance of the scaleup in their product–market. The way to entrench that dominance can take many forms.

- Sometimes the scaleup needs to build up their sales force even further.

- Sometimes it needs to embark on international expansion

- Sometimes it needs to launch an adjacent product.

- Sometimes the best way of entrenching dominance is to buy a key competitor.

This is why the size of a Series C round varies much more than the Series A or Series B. I am hesitant to attach any range to it.

DOUG: Does this also mean that sophomore scaleups are not always ticking the same boxes to raise a series C?

ROLAND: Investment criteria definitely become more specific in Series C and beyond. As does the goal of the investment. This is a natural consequence of the scaleup growing up. Of it embracing its own identity and finding its true strengths in the marketplace. As a consequence, there is no standard prescription for how it should develop further. It all depends on its circumstances.

DOUG: It reminds me of college freshmen and sophomores all studying the same curriculum. But juniors start specializing in different streams. And seniors may only study electives to round off their education.

ROLAND: That is a great analogy. As mentioned earlier, the key is that the scaleup has established some dominance. At least in one beachhead of the mainstream market. Investors must have the confidence that the scaleup is here to stay. ThatIt further investments will help entrench that dominance. That the scaleup will not be run over by incumbent competition.

DOUG: What if the scaleup has not been able to establish dominance on any market?

ROLAND: That brings us to the other purpose of a series C. It is also used often for fixing problems left from Series B or even A.

DOUG: So our junior scaleup that has not been able to dominate a mainstream beachhead yet. Can it use series C money to try again?

ROLAND: Yes, if investors still believe the scaleup has a good chance of succeeding this time. And of course they will take a discount on the valuation. As well as impose management changes. All to increase their chances of getting a positive return out of the investment. You can imagine that this is not the best scenario for the original founders.

DOUG: So let us hope our scaleup has followed most of our prescriptions so far, and is raising a successful series C!

6

Conclusion: Mid-Stage Scaleups

DOUG: We have now covered the first half of the Scaleup Roadmap. Or the Scaleup Rollercoaster. What are some parting words you want to leave with us today?

ROLAND: The key message we want to impart is that you need to manage a scaleup in a different way than a startup. But also in a different way than an incumbent corporation. It is its own animal with its own specific challenges and best practices.

DOUG: And the consequence of that is that the founders need to change and adapt. If they want to stay in charge of their venture. That has been my key insight in working with you on this book.

ROLAND: Oh thank you, indeed a crucial message to founders as well. Not only the macro change from startup founder to scaleup leader. But also the shorter term buildup of new competences for each phase of the scaleup roadmap.

DOUG: Summarize this book in a list of specific actions for scaleup founders. What would you have them start with?

ROLAND: Well, following Warren Buffet's advice, of course I could put no more than five priorities on that list. It depends on the exact phase the scaleup is in. But in general, I would recommend:

1. Gain a complete understanding what phase of the startup-scaleup-incumbent curve your venture is in. Make certain your team aligns on this.

2. Follow the recommendations for each phase in this book. Identify possible blind spots for the phase you are in.

3. Start running disciplined quarterly sessions for priority-setting, and avoid setting new priorities in-between.

4. Use these sessions to work towards a fully filled out One Page Strategic Plan. Share it with your stakeholders.

5. Finally, get an external coach or facilitator. They can help the team adopt scaling best practices and coach them through blind spots.

DOUG: Where can they find such an external coach, or what should they do if they want further help?

ROLAND: We are happy to recommend a fitting coach from the worldwide Gazelles network or other coaches we trust and have worked with.

I would encourage any tech scaleup founders—freshman stage and beyond—to drop us a line:

- mailto:roland@scaleupallies.com

- `mailto:doug@scaleupallies.com`

Other than that, follow our blog and social media postings and be on the lookout for our next book.

DOUG: We look forward to seeing you break through the challenges your tech company faces. And helping out based on the Scaleup Rollercoaster Roadmap.

7

Next Volume: Late-Stage Scaleups

DOUG: We are now working on Volume II of *Scaling Silicon Valley Style.* What can people expect in that book?

ROLAND: The sequel book will cover the late-stage scaleup journey: Junior Scaleups, Senior Scaleups and what we could call "Graduate Scaleups." Companies that have reached product-market dominance and have become incumbents themselves.

DOUG: Other than the timing in the journey, what is going to be different for these more mature scaleups?

ROLAND: The key difference is that a junior scaleup has made a decided breakthrough into the mass market. It has "crossed the chasm" (Moore, 2013) and has a solid chance to reach product-market-dominance. That means more conscious attacks on incumbents (mastering disruption). But also ensuring that no-one else can attack your own position (mastering defense).

DOUG: What changes will we see in this later stage? When looking at the relative importance of people management, strategy, execution and cash?

ROLAND: Good question. I have several thoughts about that:

1. People management will be more about managing layers of managers. About getting large amounts of people to work together in effective ways. Less about the top team.

2. Strategy will be ever more about making tough choices and embracing who you are (or have become).

3. On execution, the team will have learned many of the disciplines already. The challenge will be delegating decisions to autonomous business units and shared functions.

4. With regards to cash, there will be a strong shift away from attracting more investor money. There is going to be more and more pressure to show that you can make a profit.

DOUG: What stories are we looking to include?

ROLAND: Just like in this book, we hope to include interesting stories from our pasts in ten-odd scaleups. But we also want to open it up to stories from current scaleups. If your scaleup is (or was recently) between series C and an exit or incumbent status, then please drop me a line on roland@scaleupallies.com so that we can plan for an interview.

DOUG: Readers, as we write this in Q1/2018, the sequel book is scheduled to be available for preorder in Q1/2019 and fully published from Q2/2019. You can expect excerpts of it to appear on our blog at www.scaleupallies.com from Q3/2018.

List of Abbreviations

3HAG Three-year Highly Achievable Goal. A highly effective planning methodology from Shannon Byrne Susko to break down long-term goals into annual objectives and quarterly rocks.

BHAG® Big Hairy Audacious Goal. The unreasonable long term goal people set to provide a compass and a horizon for a journey much longer than the foreseeable future (10–30 years). BHAG® is a registered trademark by Jim Collins and Jerry Porras Collins and Porras, 2002.

FACe Gazelles' Functional Accountability Chart. A tool to clarify which executives are responsible for what functional objectives, and to avoid gaps and overlaps in the executive team.

IPO Initial Public Offering. The first time a scaleup lists its shares on a public stock exchange for sale to the general public.

OKR Objectives and Key Results. A methodology to ensure all employees have goals aligned with the vision of the company.

OPPP One Page Personal Plan. Worksheet for scaleup executives to reconnect with their personal mission in life.

OPSP One Page Strategic Plan. Gazelles' key strategic planning tool for scaleup companies.

PACe Gazelles' Process Accountability Chart. A tool to clarify which executives are responsible for what cross-functional processes, and to ensure all are covered in the executive team.

SWOT Strengths, Weaknesses, Opportunities and Threats. A strategic tool to gather suggestions from middle management before top management adjusts their strategy.

SWT Strengths, Weaknesses, Trends. Gazelles' tool for top management to align on the foundations they "have to work with" before deciding on adjusting their strategies.

VC Venture Capital(ist). A fund that invests money attracted from outside investors into speculative growth companies.

Works Cited

Blank, S.

    2005   *The Four Steps to the Epiphany: Successful Strategies for Products that Win*, 2nd ed. K and S Ranch Inc., Palo Alto.

    2015   *What Do I Do Now? The Startup Lifecycle*, https://steveblank.com/2015/02/12/what-do-i-do-now/ (on Jan. 4, 2018).

Brandt, R. L.

    2011   "Birth of a Salesman—The Saturday Essay", *Wall Street Journal*, Oct 15th.

Burgelman, R. A.

    2002   *Strategy is Destiny: How Strategy-Making Shapes a Company's Future*, Free Press.

Byrne Susko, S.

    2014   *The Metronome Effect: The Journey To Predictable Profit*, Advantage Media Group, Charleston, NC.

    2018   *3HAG WAY: the strategic execution system that ensures your strategy is not a wild ass guess.*

Calacanis, J.

    2017   "All #AskJason: Failing after Product-Market-Fit", *This Week in Startups (podcast)*, 735, http://thisweekinstartups.com/all-ask-jason-05-2017/.

CB Insights

    2017   *Venture Capital Funnel Shows Odds of Becoming a Unicorn Are Less than 1%*, https://www.cbinsights.com/research/venture-capital-funnel-2/ (on Jan. 5, 2018).

Collins, J.

    2001   *Good to Great: Why Some Companies Make the Leap... and Others Don't*, Random House, Chicago.

Collins, J. and J. I. Porras

    2002   *Built to Last: Successful Habits of Visionary Companies*, Harper Paperbacks, http://www.amazon.de/dp/0060516402.

Covey, S. R.

    2013   *The Seven Habits of Highly Successful People: Powerful Lessons in Personal Change*, Simon & Schuster.

First Round Review and M. Graham

    2015   *'Give Away Your Legos' and Other Commandments for Scaling Startups*, http://firstround.com/review/give-away-your-legos-and-other-commandments-for-scaling-startups/ (on Jan. 27, 2018).

First Round Review and R. Sutton

    2015   *The Do's and Don'ts of Rapid Scaling for Startups*, http://firstround.com/review/The-Dos-and-Donts-of-Rapid-Scaling-for-Startups/ (on Jan. 27, 2018).

Fleming, S.

    2007   *Painkillers*, http://academicvc.com/2007/06/04/painkillers/ (on Dec. 22, 2017).

Gazelles

    2015a "Execution: Rockefeller Habits Checklist™", https://gazelles.com/resources/growth-tools.

    2015b "People: Function Accountability Chart (FACe)", https://gazelles.com/resources/growth-tools.

Gerber, M.

    2004   *The E-Myth Revisited: Why Most Small Businesses Don't Work and What to Do About It*, Santa Rosa.

Goldsmith, M. and M. Reiter

    2007   *What Got You Here Won't Get You There. How Successful People Become Even More Successful!*, Hyperion, New York City.

Griffin, T.

    2017   *12 Things about Product-Market Fit*, https://a16z.com/2017/
            02/18/12-things-about-product-market-fit/ (on Feb. 3, 2018).

Halligan, B.

    2016   *HubSpot's Playbook for Going From Startup to Scale-up*, https:
            //readthink.com.

Hargreaves, R.

    2017   *Warren Buffett on the Importance of Moats*, http://www.nasdaq.
            com/article/warren-buffett-on-the-importance-of-moats-
            cm767018 (on Feb. 3, 2018).

Harnish, V.

    2002   *Mastering the Rockefeller Habits: What You Must Do to Increase
            the Value of Your Growing Firm*, 1st ed. Gazelles, Inc.

    2005   *Rockefeller Habits with Verne Harnish*, tech. rep., Gazelles.

    2008   *Four Decisions: People, Strategy, Execution, Cash*, www.gazell
            es.com (on July 7, 2016).

    2014   *Scaling Up: How a Few Companies Make It... and Why the Rest
            Don't (Rockefeller Habits 2.0)*, 1st ed. Gazelles, Inc., Ashburn,
            VA.

Hoffman, R.

    2017a   "Escape the Competition, with Peter Thiel, Co-founder &
            CEO of Paypal", *Masters of Scale Podcast*, 1, 11.

    2017b   *Masters of Scale Podcast. A WaitWhat Original Podcast in As-
            sociation with Stitcher.* www.mastersofscale.com.

2018   "How to Price your Product to Scale, with Payal Kadakia, Founder & Chair of ClassPass", *Masters of Scale Podcast*, 2, 19, https://mastersofscale.com/payal-kadakia-how-to-price-your-product-to-scale/.

Horowitz, B.

2014   *The Hard Thing about Hard Things. Building a Business When There Are No Easy Answers*, Harper Business.

Lamorte, B.

2016   "Objective and Key Results", http://www.okrs.com/2016/12/bens-white-paper/.

Linowes, J. S.

1999   *A Summary of "Crossing the Chasm"*, tech. rep., Parker Hill Technology, https://ewthoff.home.xs4all.nl/.../Summary%20Crossing%20the%20Chasm.pdf.

Lublin, J. S.

2017   "Overconfident CEOs: their era is ending", *Wall Street Journal*, March 8th.

Marmer, M., B. Lasse Hermann, E. Dogruitan, and R. Berman

2011   *Startup genome report. A new framework for understanding why startups succeed.* Tech. rep., Startup Genome LLC, San Francisco, www.startupgenome.com.

Moore, G.

2011   *Escape Velocity: Free Your Company's Future From the Pull of the Past*, Harper Collins.

Moore, G.

    2013   *Crossing the Chasm. Marketing and Selling Disruptive Products to Mainstream Customers.* 3rd ed.

Osterwalder, A. and Y. Pigneur

    2009   *Business Model Generation: A Handbook for Visionaries, Game Changers, and Challengers,* John Wiley & Sons Ltd.

Picken, J. C.

    2017   "From founder to CEO: An entrepreneur's roadmap", *Business Horizons.*

Putorti, J.

    2016   *8 Lessons Learned from Political Startups: A look back on working to make a difference from 2009–2016,* https://medium.com/startup-grind/.

Ries, E.

    2011   *The Lean Startup: How Today's Entrepreneurs Use Continuous Innovation to Create Radically Successful Businesses,* Crown Business.

Siebelink, R.

    2009   *Apt Metrics, Astute Measures. A Strategic Approach to Performance Management,* Lulu Press.

    2017a   *Fewer Markets, Bigger Profits. An Interview with Pieter Mees (Founder/CTO of Zentrick),* https://medium.com/@cyberroland/fewer-markets-bigger-profits.

2017b   *Scaling Up Sales — Without the Slumps. An Interview with Jon Kondo (Founder/CEO of OpsPanda),* https://medium.com/ @cyberroland/scaling-up-sales-without-the-slumps (on Oct. 12, 2017).

Startup Genome, Crunchbase, and Orb Intelligence

2017   *Global Startup Ecosystem Report 2017,* tech. rep., www.startu pgenome.com.

Townsend, T.

2015   "Reid Hoffman: The First Three Stages of Blitzscaling", *Inc Magazine* (Nov. 2015), https://www.inc.com.

Tsotsis, A.

2011   "Dave McClure On 500 Startups: «If Sequoia Is The Yankees, We're The Oakland A's»", *TechCrunch.com,* April 10th.

Vangool, J.

2011   "DesignThinkers: Rei Inamoto", *Upper Case Magazine,* www.uppercasemagazine.com.

Wasserman, N.

2008   "The Founder's Dilemma", *Harvard Business Review,* 86, 2.

Wickman, G.

2013   *Traction. Get a Grip on your Business. Expanded Edition.* 3rd ed. BenBella Books, Dallas, TX.

Yeh, C. and C. McCann

    2015   *Blitzscaling: 16 lessons on scaling from Eric Schmidt, Reid Hoffman, Marissa Mayer, Brian Chesky, Diane Greene, Jeff Weiner, and more.* https://medium.com/cs183c-blitzscaling-class-collection/ (on July 11, 2016).

Index

NOTES

NOTES

NOTES

Dear Reader,

I hope you have enjoyed this book. Other readers will discover it more easily through reviews from readers like you.

Will you do us and other readers a big favor and post a quick review?

https://r13k.co/bookreview

It will be of tremendous help for everyone. Even one sentence is OK!

Thank you for your help!

Roland

PS any questions? Please reach out to roland@scaleupallies.com

46090291R10134